Holy Transfiguration Monastery

The Monks of Mt. Tabor
(Byzantine-Ukrainian Catholic)

17001 Tomki Rd., Redwood Valley, CA 95470
(707) 485-8959

Why be a Christian?

Why be a Christian?

ROSEMARY HAUGHTON

J. B. LIPPINCOTT COMPANY
Philadelphia and New York

First Edition

Library of Congress Catalog Card No.: 68-24192

This book is set in 12 on 14 Baskerville
Printed in Great Britain

Contents

I

WHY BE A CHRISTIAN?

I

WHY BE A CHRISTIAN?

THE TITLE OF THIS book can be taken two ways. It might be the title of a book that shows a Christian how to get other people to see some sense in being Christian—or at least to see why it can make sense for *someone* to be a Christian, even if they don't want to be one themselves. Or it could try to answer a really personal question—why am *I* a Christian?

In fact, this book is intended to be helpful in both ways, but the second is more important. It is more important, because no one is likely to be able to 'put over' the Christian idea to other people in an intelligent and effective way until they have faced up to the basic question: why should *I* be a Christian?

Many people who are brought up as Christians don't ask themselves this question at all. They take their Christian faith for granted. Sometimes this is a good thing. There are many marvellous Christians who are much too busy living the Gospel to have any need to stop and wonder *why* they believe. Their faith grows and develops as their lives grow and develop, and they never notice what's happening, they don't stop to inspect the growth.

But sometimes this 'taking for granted' is not good because it simply means that a person has never let his Christianity grow up at all. It's still a childish, un-thought-out belief, and it doesn't affect his *real* life in any important way. Apart from the fact that maybe he goes to church, and says he believes certain things, he might just as well not call himself a Christian at all.

But, either way, it is becoming more and more difficult to take your Christianity for granted. We live in a world that is not Christian. Most of the people we live with and work with are not Christians. Even if they were baptized their notions of what Christianity is are often so hazy that for all practical purposes they aren't Christians at all. And besides the many who are simply 'not Christians', there is also quite a number (and it's growing) who are *anti*-Christian. They think that Christianity is not only nonsense but a bad influence, and should not be taught in State schools, or 'advertised' by radio and television services, discussions, and so on. They don't normally want churches closed by law (in fact one of the reasons they dislike Christianity is because they say Christians want to take away people's freedom to worship or not worship as they please) but they would do a lot to make people realize that Christianity is false. And some of them are highly intelligent, sensitive people, who work very hard to help others, who are self-sacrificing, even heroic.

Somewhere between these really convinced anti-Christians and the simply 'non-Christians' there are also a great many people—especially young ones—who don't fight Christianity because they think it isn't worth fighting. They simply reject it. They think it is a ridiculous, obsolete religion, they will scarcely discuss it because they regard it as so futile it isn't worth the effort. Their attitude is not that Christianity is bad, but that Christianity is *over*. What they care about is the future, and in their eyes Christianity *has* no future. There are a great many people who feel like this in the universities, in colleges and training schools of all kinds, and also among young people in all kinds of jobs.

Therefore, many people who have been brought up as Christians will leave school and find themselves in a world full of people who mostly think their religion is, at best, a nice, comforting but unimportant belief and, at worst, a ridiculous and dangerous madness. In that case they must be either very thick-skinned and very stupid, or perhaps very saintly indeed, if sooner or later they don't find themselves forced to ask 'Are they right? Is there really any sense in it? *Why* am I a Christian? What possible reason can I find for going on being one?'

When someone finds himself asking questions of this kind—or even feeling he should ask them, but not quite wanting to—there are two alternative things he can do. The first is to regard these questions as temptations against faith, and as something to be fought and resisted.

He feels that even to ask such questions is to admit defeat. There is a certain sense in this, because Christianity is not an intellectual system—you don't become a Christian in the same way that you find the answer to a sum. I shall say more about this later, but it is true that to try to work out 'doubts' or 'temptations against faith' as if you were simply trying to correct mistakes in arithmetic is foolish and unrealistic. To do that *would* be to admit defeat.

The other way to think about such questions is to see them as a necessary part of one's development as a Christian. Trying to answer them means trying to see what it means to be an adult Christian, and not a child, with a child's unquestioning belief. In fact it is true to say that whether you do it consciously or not, you have to work out these questions in your life if your faith is to be something real, something living and dynamic, and not simply a set of statements you say you believe —which isn't really faith in any proper sense.

On the other hand it is obviously better to begin thinking about all this before it actually comes up and hits you. The middle of an argument with non-Christians (especially if they tell you a lot of things you never knew before) is not the easiest place to start re-thinking what Christianity means. Besides, one doesn't try to grow up spiritually just because someone says 'you're wrong'. It would be just as important to do so even if everyone around were Christian.

So it is useful to go into these questions in a fairly leisurely way, at a time when one has a chance to think and discuss with other people who are facing the same problems, or have faced them in the past.

This book can't give the *answers* to these questions. In a sense there *are* no answers. Christianity is a *life*, not an argument. But what a book can do is to show the sort of thing Christianity is, and—almost as important —what it isn't. Nobody can give another person faith but somebody can, as it were, put one in a position where one can see what faith is, and what it demands. Then each one can decide, and it is the deciding that counts. It is a special kind of deciding, as I shall discuss later.

Usually, when people are studying a subject, the writer or teacher or lecturer tries to present the facts as impartially as possible. He has his own opinions, but unless he is very conceited he knows his conclusions may be wrong, or at least may need to be adjusted. His chief concern is that his students should have all the materials available, so that they can discover the truth for themselves, with him as a guide.

Someone who writes a book about Christianity or teaches it is not in quite the same position. From one point of view, he is doing the same job as anyone else—presenting a subject. When I write about Christianity *I* am giving *you*, the reader, the relevant facts, as truthfully as I can, both about Christian teaching and history and about non-Christian ideas and their value and importance. Also, I know I am liable to make mistakes, my opinions could be wrong, I might change them, and certainly they will develop as time goes on. Other

Christians might explain it all differently, or even disagree with me flatly about a number of things. My concern is not to persuade you that I am right but to put you in a position to discuss the truth.

But that is the difficulty. Truth is not just facts. Truth is basically about people—it is the knowledge of what human beings really are, and that means the knowledge of what makes them what they are. But clearly this kind of truth cannot be known just by thinking. It can only be discovered by living, living with other people—not just being around with them, but really sharing yourself with them. This is how you 'get to know' yourself. Truth, in this sense, means the sharing of life, the 'openness' of people to each other. When people can trust each other, when they don't hide things or cheat each other, then the relationship between them is a 'true' one. They are discovering truth, not only *about* but *in* each other. *This* is the kind of truth that Christianity is about, as well as being about facts. And facts are, if you think about it, only useful in order to make people able to understand the world and each other, and live together more easily in it, so that they will be able to discover the deeper truth.

So the truth the Christian wants to know, and wants other people to know, is something that can only be known by 'giving yourself' to it, as people who love each other give themselves. In fact this kind of truth is so mixed up with love that you can't separate them. Christian truth is something you discover by loving, and love is not a thing you can be impartial about. That would be as if you decided whom you wanted to marry by listing your requirements for an ideal wife or husband, and then impartially examining the available people until you found someone who seemed to fit your list, more or less. You might say that a marriage decided on like that was sensible, but you would not suppose there was much love involved.

And a convinced Christian is, basically, someone in love. That is the reason why Christians are Christians themselves, and also why they want other people to be Christians, too—to share their experience of love.

I can try to show what is involved in this truth which is love—the kind of effect it has on people, the demands it makes. All these are matters of fact, and if they are to be useful they must be presented as clearly and accurately as possible, and as impartially. If I tried to pretend, or cover up difficulties, I would be admitting (to myself at least) that Christianity is not true *enough* to be shown clearly, but needs to be dressed up to look better than it is. But a really convinced Christian wouldn't see any point in pretending about his faith—he knows it can stand any amount of inspection. So to be impartial and honest is simply the *only* way of doing justice to the thing we are discussing.

No Christian is in the least impartial about the thing he has discovered and wants another to discover. If I were impartial, I wouldn't be writing this book. Anyone who writes a book like this, or teaches other people about Christianity, *is* partisan, *is* biased, is *certain* he's right —right about where the truth (in the sense described above) lies, though not necessarily about the best way to present it.

All this sounds very 'personal'. But in fact this particular job *has* to be done 'personally'.

Just as Christianity cannot be presented impartially by a Christian, so it cannot be taught 'impersonally'. It is about love, about sharing, about *life*, and life is lived by people, not by disembodied ideas.

Christianity has always been handed on from one to another *personally*. Even if the preacher is addressing a whole crowd, still he is a person, talking to people--he is talking to them, as people, he isn't just giving some facts. Faith is something you 'catch' from someone who has it, even though you don't know them privately, even though it is put down in a book, not spoken. Because this truth about life, in life, is the discovery of what underlies *all* life, something bigger than any one person, but something that people share in. This is what we call God.

God is extremely personal, he is what makes each human being personal, makes them really themselves, and not anyone else. And it is by being personal—being ourselves—that we can really share. Or you can put it the other way, and say that it is by sharing—giving ourselves—that we become really ourselves. (Think of people you know. Which ones seem to be most 'complete' and interesting—the generous and loving or the suspicious and withdrawn?) So the handing on of the Christian message is very much a personal matter. But the person who hands on the message is not handing on himself, although *his* self is the only way he has of sharing the truth with *your* self. The handing on of the message is really what Christians have always called 'preaching the good news'. And this news is not about the preacher, it is news about Jesus Christ. He is the only possible reason for being a Christian; yet we can only hear the news from someone who has heard it himself and accepted it and begun to live in a new kind of life.

II

A LIFE OR A WAY OF LIFE?

II

A LIFE OR A WAY OF LIFE?

IF I WANT to find out why I should be a Christian I want to know what Christianity *is*. And first of all that means clearing out of the way quite a few irrelevancies. A lot of talk about Christianity is as if people talked about a certain family only by discussing the size and shape of their house, their furniture, their clothes, their food, what time they get up or go to bed, their tastes in music or where they go for a holiday. If you are interested in that family, all this *is* interesting, and facts like these do tell you a lot about what kind of family it is. But if that is *all* you discuss you can only get an incomplete idea of what sort of life goes on in that family, what makes these people tick.

And yet a lot of us do talk about other people in just that way. If you listen to conversations in buses, or suddenly 'tune in' to your own conversations, you will hear human beings discussed as if their lives could be adequately represented by comments on their clothes, their incomes and their table-manners. In the same way you hear people talking about Christianity—or more often about particular Christian Churches—as if the 'furniture' of Christianity were the thing itself. The type of worship Christians go in for, the causes they support (or don't), the parties they vote for, the kind of people who lead them, the nationalities that bred them, the customs they stick to, the 'language' they use, and how their moral standards compare with those of non-believers—these are the kind of things one hears discussed.

All these things are important, even extremely important, if you want to get a clear idea of the sort of thing Christianity is. It is by the way people behave in everyday life that we can tell what they are like, at least until we get to know them really intimately. When we do, we can see that particular bits of behaviour are often misleading, since the 'real' person we've got to know isn't like this. And it is the 'real' person that we really want to know—even though his behaviour isn't something separate but is himself. I *am* the way I behave, but my behaviour, all the same, may be *un*real in some ways, because it contradicts something in myself which I (and my best friends) feel is truly 'me'.

It is the same with Christianity. We can only know Christianity by the Church—that is, by the behaviour of a lot of people who call themselves Christians. How else would we know it? But as we get to know it better we realize that some of the behaviour of Christians isn't completely 'real', that some of it may even be contradicting what we have come to recognize as *really* Christian.

How can we tell what is really Christian and what is not? Isn't it just that we pick out certain kinds of behaviour that we happen to like and say 'That's really Christian', and other behaviour that we don't like, and say 'That's unchristian'? Or if we don't like Christianity we can pick out types of behaviour in Christians that we like and say, 'That's good, but of course it isn't anything to do with Christianity, they are just good people, and would have been good anyway'.

The way to discover what to call 'really Christian' is rather the same as the way you might set out to discover what a family was like. If someone asked you, 'What are those new people down the road *really* like?', you would try to give some idea of the quality of living that went on in the house. You might have seen them moving in, and thought 'What terrible furniture!' or 'What noisy, filthy children!' But unless you were a very superficial and prejudiced person you would not condemn them on these things alone, you would form your judgment on the whole human situation. You would describe your feelings about them as people whom you had actually *met*, about the kind of relationships between members of the family, the sort of welcome you got when you called. And you might find that the general atmosphere of warmth and liveliness and affection quite outweighed the ugliness of the furniture or the scruffiness of the people, and even the occasional rows and general disorderliness. You might find these drawbacks hard to put up with, and yet worth putting up with, for the sake of the 'real' quality of their family life. And if someone challenged you, and said, 'But they are so noisy and dirty, and the children are rude and they break things', you might have to admit all that, and you would probably find it quite difficult to persuade someone who had taken a dislike to them that they were 'really' marvellous people. In fact you would find it very difficult to say what you meant by 'really'. Because, after all, the dirt and the noise are just as 'real' as the kindness, in one sense. And to many people they are *more* real.

It would work the other way, too. If the new neighbours were pleasant, well-behaved people, whose house was attractive and whose manners were charming, you might yet find that on closer acquaintance you didn't feel you specially wanted to go to the house, except for the odd party. (I don't mean that a well-behaved family is necessarily dull or unwelcoming, or a noisy, dirty one attractive. Many noisy, dirty families are also quarrelsome, selfish and unkind. Maybe it isn't their fault, but there it is. And 'respectable' people are often warm-hearted, generous and gay. I simply mean that their exterior habits and behaviour, though obvious, and obviously important, are not in the end the things that make you feel you want to be with these people, or not. What attracts you, or doesn't, is the *life* of the family, the quality of their living together.)

It works the same way with the Church. In the first chapter I said that Christianity is a life, and this really is the essential thing about it. But when people talk about Christianity as a life they often mean simply a *way* of life. Christianity does have a way of life, just as the two families I described have a way of life. And in each case you can easily imagine that if they had had more or less money, or lived in a different country, or had more or less education, their way of life would have been altered. And this alteration would also alter, probably, the way they felt and thought about each other in the family. In that case it would alter their *life*, as well as their *way* of life. But the two are distinct, even though you can't separate them. So when people talk about Christianity as a way of life they are talking about the way Christians in each place and time try to discover and *live* the kind of life they have. And of course the way people think and feel in each time and place is not an extra, it is what makes them *themselves*. So Christians are the kind of Christians they are because of when and where they live and how they are brought up and so on, like everyone else.

But in each particular time and place, each particular 'way of being', there is this life which people are trying to know, to discover. They can only do it according to the ways of thinking and feeling that are theirs—that are actually *them*—but this life isn't, itself, the *way* of life by which it is known and lived, any more than the *way* of life of those two families was all there was to them, as communities.

Food and clothing (and all the rest of a way of life) are not only necessary to go on living, they are also the way people stay alive at all. There is no other way. But all the same 'the life is more than the food, the body is more than the clothes'.

So Christianity *is* a way of life and we can't and shouldn't try to separate out the 'life' part, as if we could reduce Christianity to a sort of dehydrated extract that could be mixed with whatever materials were available to form the contemporary soup. The life of a person is himself, and himself is the way he lives. If you try to strip off the way he lives you don't have pure 'life' left, but the opposite—you have a corpse. And Christianity is a life, and it is always the same life, just as people are always recognizably human, however extreme the differences between different kinds of human.

But the Christian claim is not that Christianity is *a* life, but that the thing that makes Christians Christian is *the* life, just life itself.

This is such a peculiar claim, and so difficult to pin down, that we generally slide over it. We say, quite rightly, that many people who are not Christians are just as good as those who are. In that case, they must have this 'life' in them. If that is so, what is Christian about it? In other words, why be a Christian? It seems that we are back where we started, and so we are, but with one distinct advantage. We can now see that if we are going to discover what Christianity is and accept it or refuse it, we must look beyond the Christian *way* of life and try to get the 'feel' of the life itself. And if we do that we can recognize that 'feel' in *any* circumstances, Christian or not. We shall then be in a position to say what, if anything, is Christian about *life*, and therefore how being a Christian puts you in touch with this life.

If we are claiming that life itself is in some sense to be found in Christianity, and nowhere else, we are moving beyond the idea of '*a*' life as I first suggested we could feel it in two sample families. It begins to look as if one family's 'real' life *was* real in a sense that the other's wasn't. The second family *lacked* something, lacked the quality of *livingness* which made the first, for all their unpleasant habits, obviously worthwhile and attractive to be with. The idea of 'life', rather than 'a life' means, then, that what draws people together, gives them a sense of warmth and 'aliveness', is in fact life. It is the thing, whatever it is, that 'makes alive'. And if we are withdrawn, isolated, repelled, that is because we have failed to 'get at' the source of life. Something (in us or in the other person or in both) is getting in the way, is shutting us off from living.

This is precisely the kind of feeling one does get from some people. They make one feel constrained, depressed or uncomfortable in their company, even though they may be reasonably pleasant and polite. It may perfectly well be one's own fault, or nobody's fault, but feeling like this makes it possible to realize without difficulty that this is a situation of being *less* alive, certainly less alive than you feel in the company of other people with whom you get on well.

This idea of 'liveness' is important. It isn't easy to

describe but it is perfectly easy to recognize. It comes in moments of excitement or pleasure, sometimes through danger—which is why people will even make artificial dangers for themselves, whether it's the big-dipper or mountain climbing. A magnificent view can give it to you, or a new discovery, an idea that suddenly comes clear, or—less pleasantly—a furious temper. But the thing that gives this feeling of liveness most surely is meeting another person, or people, with whom you realize you can feel at home and happy. It is as if barriers had been broken down and you are aware that you are *sharing* something. Whatever it is, is 'between' you and the other or others, but also you are *in* it, it is a different kind of experience from anything else. You feel relaxed, exhilarated, eager and yet peaceful. Yet it can be almost painful. And besides all this, if you stop to think about it (which you don't usually) you realize that you feel much more *yourself*, much more what you *really are*, than usual.

This experience of being really oneself and *at the same time* sharing in something bigger than oneself is what I called being 'alive'. There is no other word for it. It is something that everyone wants. If they haven't been able to find it in love and companionship and the experience of beauty and discovery (all these experiences are linked) they will look for it in *any* experience that gives even a brief sense of this 'liveness'—drugs or violence or quick, promiscuous sex. Some people get a kick out of hurting other people, or exercising power in some other way. These ways of feeling alive don't last, because there is really nothing *to* last, which is why people always want more and more and get more and more desperate. But however much of a dead-end this kind of experience may be, it does show the way in which people desire the experience of 'liveness' and will do almost anything to get it. A more harmless but still unsatisfying way of getting it is by imaginary experiences, derived from stories or films or phantasies people invent for themselves. People who take this way can become more and more engrossed in their dream world, which becomes more 'alive' for them than the real world.

But however you get the experience of 'liveness', and whether it is really one that can satisfy you and grow or just a fleeting and disappointing hint, the important thing about it is the fact that it matters because it makes you feel that you are fully (or at least *more*) alive, and that this liveness is your *own* life. It comes from 'inside' you, somehow, even though it is triggered off by something 'outside'.

(It is impossible to talk about things like this without using rather clumsy metaphors. Of course this experience is no more really 'in' than 'out' of you, your experience is simply *you*. But 'spatial' metaphors like this help to make clearer the meaning of ideas that have nothing to do with space.)

This feeling of liveness, of being really oneself, is the experience that shows what Christianity means by *life*. This life is what we experience, hazily and briefly, at moments of heightened awareness. This isn't all there is to it, of course, but it is a good enough place to begin.

In fact it is the obvious place to begin, because the best definition of what Christianity is for is the one in St John's Gospel, in which these words are used to express the mission of Christ: 'I came so that you should have *life*, and have *more* of it'.

III

'LIVING AND PARTLY LIVING'

III

'LIVING AND PARTLY LIVING'

THE TITLE OF this chapter is a quotation from T. S. Eliot's play *Murder in the Cathedral.* It is spoken by the chorus of the ordinary women of Canterbury, as they express their feeling about their life, its satisfactions and fears and hopes, going on under the continuous surface of routine jobs that have to be done, because that's what life is like. Yet that isn't all there is to life. Most of the time we feel we are only 'partly living', and we aren't content with that; yet at the same time we are rather afraid of anything more. Being only partly alive is more comfortable than the stress and danger of real life, which is full of unknown and threatening things, in a future which we cannot penetrate. We don't really want anything drastic to happen.

'We do not wish anything to happen.
Seven years we have lived quietly,

Succeeded in avoiding notice,
Living and partly living.
There have been oppression and luxury,
There have been poverty and licence,
There has been minor injustice.
Yet we have gone on living,
Living and partly living.
Sometimes the corn has failed us,
Sometimes the harvest is good,
One year is a year of rain,
Another a year of dryness.
One year the apples are abundant,
Another year the plums are lacking.
Yet we have gone on living,
Living and partly living.
We have kept the feasts, heard the Masses,
We have brewed beer and cyder
Gathered wood against the winter,
Talked at the corners of the fire,
Talked at the corners of the streets,
Talked not always in whispers,
Living and partly living.'

It isn't just cowardice that makes people cling to the habits and customs that they know, if they stop to think about it, are only 'partly living'. We need these customs, rules, routines, in order to be people who can live fully, when the opportunity comes. But the *kind* of 'partly living' we go in for makes all the difference. It makes the difference between experiencing 'life' as whole and growing, continuing even under the surface of 'partly living', and gradually charging it with full life, or experiencing it only as fleeting moments of liveness, with deserts of futility in between.

In the last chapter I mentioned a number of different ways of 'feeling alive'; not all of them involved behaviour which we could possibly call 'good'. Yet all of these, and many others, are ways in which people can have a real experience that can best be described as feeling 'alive' or feeling 'really oneself'. Each is an experience of 'realness'. Some of them seem to be self-defeating—the way in which they happen doesn't allow the experience to grow, to extend itself into other parts of life so that the person becomes 'living' rather than 'partly living'. If you lose your temper and have a huge row, you feel 'real' enough, and it is really quite a pleasurable and exhilarating sensation while it lasts. But when it's over it usually leaves you flat and miserable and apprehensive. Even while you are in the middle of the row, you may have a notion at the back of your mind that you are going to regret it. A person who takes drugs feels terrifically alive and life is full of intense meaning while he's 'high', but when the drug wears off he feels horrible, he can hardly bear himself. He tries to sleep as much as possible, he drags through the hours, somehow, until he can get his next fix. The sensation that was so real while it lasted has no power to give meaning to the rest of life. On the contrary, it makes ordinary living almost impossible. And the fear of the inevitable awakening gives even the 'high' periods a background of dread, so that the addict wants more and more of the drug, to make him forget what lies ahead.

To some extent the same thing applies to sex as a way of feeling real and alive. People who use sex *simply* as a way of getting a personal experience of intense pleasure and release are not able to use the experience to give meaning to the rest of their lives. They can talk about it and think about it, and so extend the experience, in a way, but this talking and thinking is simply another, less complete way of escaping from the full awareness of the rest of life. It doesn't help any other kind of activity to seem more important or interesting. Rather the contrary. But when a sexual relationship is a personal one—even if it isn't a lasting one—it can carry over the experience of liveness into other parts of living. This happens because in that case it is an experience *shared*. People who go for sex alone don't *share* the experience; the other person's body means little more to them than the drug addict's syringe or pill. But someone who *shares* sex experience is aware of a person and there is a relationship between them, even if it doesn't amount to much. To that extent what they feel about each other will affect the way they feel about the rest of their life. The rest of life will be at least 'partly living' and not simply futile and dead.

But if the couple are really fond of each other their experience of sex as a shared experience will affect their lives more and more. The more they really care about each other the more they will want to share *all* their lives. This is why sex, as a shared experience, only fully becomes itself when it can give the meaning of 'liveness' and 'realness' to the whole of life, even the 'partly living' bits. This is what marriage is about, and why marriage is not just legalized sex but rather the natural and proper setting for sex, if it isn't to remain stunted and only half used.

But if this is true of sex as an experience of liveness it means that if it is to be really an experience of *life*, and not just of odd moments of heightened awareness, it has to be allowed to open out and spread to other people and other parts of living. This is why the experience of 'liveness' which seems most complete and satisfactory is one which is shared with another person or people. In that case the discoveries and the feelings are shared ones, and all the greater because of that. In fact you could say that *sharing* is what the experience is about. It is an awareness of *life as shared*.

This gives us a useful standard by which to judge our own experiences. All these moments of awareness of life are real, but only those which are actually a sharing of life are able to continue and spread and change our lives. This is true even of some experiences that seem to be solitary—for instance a great scientific discovery or an impression of beauty. The scientist doesn't keep his discovery to himself. He knows he has come upon something which *needs* to be shared, whose meaning can only make sense if it *is* shared. He is excited, in the moment of break-through, by a sensation of entering into a new dimension of living, which is a shared one.

In fact the thing that has often made scientists suffer acutely has been the refusal of other people to listen, to *share* the thing they have found. And it isn't just that the scientist is sorry that people will be deprived of the benefit of his new knowledge. What he wants to share is not just the facts he has discovered but the *experience of discovery.*

If you have been moved by a play or a landscape, you normally want to share the emotion you feel. You feel frustrated by your own inability to make others, who haven't seen it, share your feeling. You bring home photographs from a holiday, and long to show them, but when you do you realize they don't mean, to the others, the experience they mean to you. But artists and writers and poets and musicians are people who *are* able to share with others their experience of the moments of awareness. That is what drives them to paint and write and compose. When you hear or see their work and respond to it, you are sharing their discovery, their awareness of living. A great painter can take a bit of 'partly living' (a chair or a landscape or a family scene) and show you the 'living' that is in it, so that always afterwards this particular bit of life really is more alive for you. Or he can teach you a new way of looking that sees more intensely than the appearance of things. This is what abstract painting tries to do. Both kinds are showing you the 'living' under the 'partly living'—the 'part' in fact that *is* living. And musicians can do the same, and so can plays.

But many modern writers and dramatists seem to be

saying to us, not 'there is living going on, even when we only know it partly'. They seem rather to be saying 'there may be living going on, but if so it might just as well not be there, because we can't get at it. Living *is only* partly living.' What has come to be called the 'kitchen sink' school of drama is basically about the way people are not able to get in touch with each other, not really able to share, though they may pretend to. It all looks fairly hopeless, it looks as if life were a series of dreary misunderstandings and pretences, leading nowhere in particular. And 'surrealist' symbolic plays like those of Beckett say this even more starkly and forcibly.

This is important, because it is to a great extent true. Many people—perhaps all of us, some of the time—feel like this. We do feel that real living is either impossible or simply a cheat, a mirage, a sensation of something that doesn't exist. People are cut off from each other, they do feel unable to say really *true* things to each other, even though they want to. Our lives are lived in a net of pretence and evasion and concealment. We deceive ourselves and each other, we distrust each other. We protect ourselves from other people by all sorts of little rules and habits, excluding, in order to feel safer, those who have different coloured skins or different beliefs or tastes in furniture or much less (or more) money than we have. But we go on with the routines, living and partly living.

All this is true, and it has always been true. People are like this. *We* are like this. But also we are people who can have the experience of real liveness, and can let it grow. This, also, has always been true. We are like this, too. Both of these things are true, but at different times in history one seems easier to believe than the other. Our particular culture has passed through experiences, like Nazism and the atomic bomb, that make it much easier to believe that people can never do anything real, can never truly *live*. In that case the only brave and human thing is to accept the moments of liveness, the 'real' moments, and live by the *sort of awareness* they give, but not try to 'read' anything into them. We should not say 'there is life', but only 'I can feel alive and that is good'. This is basically what existentialist philosophy is about, and this is why it has become so important in the years since the last war. But although this way of thinking about life helps people to cope with what can seem a hopeless situation, it doesn't altogether explain why the best kind of experience of liveness is an experience of life as shared.

If the life we discover is *really* a shared life, that means the sharing isn't just accidental. The fact that, as I suggested, this life seems to 'want' to spread and grow does seem to indicate that the sharing is of its nature. It is *that* kind of life. In fact life is something shared. This may sound obvious, but a great deal of the 'feeling' of modern life is against this, for the reasons I mentioned. Yet if you think about it you can see that even this feeling of futility, this feeling that sharing is impossible, is itself a kind of proof that life *is* shared. If the feeling of sharing life were accidental and unusual, and real sharing actually not possible, then surely people wouldn't feel so depressed about it? Why should people write plays that are a furious protest against the fact that we don't and can't share life unless, underneath, they felt that we *ought* to be able to? If the really normal human thing were *not* to share, to live separated and misunderstood, then why should we get so angry about it? Wouldn't we just accept it? Plays like those of Samuel Beckett attract audiences because they make people realize the pain of not being able to share, they make the futility and un-liveness *hurt*. If this hurting were merely painful, there would be no point in it. What makes people go to see, and think and talk about plays like these, is that realizing what is wrong actually breaks down, in some way, some of their own shut-in-ness. By hating the fact of not sharing life they become actually able to share a bit more. By reading books and seeing plays that say 'there is no sense and no meaning and no life, only pretence and futility', people are driven to put meaning and truth into their lives, even while they themselves feel there isn't any.

This happens in a rather odd way. It happens because this anger against a meaningless, shut-in life forces people to concentrate on the things they *can* do to make life better. If it's all a futile game in which no one really understands what anyone means, even what he himself means, then all that is left that can be called human or worthwhile at all is one's own face-to-face relationships with other people who happen to be there. If my life is a muddle, doomed to extinction, then at least I can be kind to *this* man I meet on the bus, I can bring a little happiness to *this* child next door, I can relieve the boredom and loneliness of *this* old lady. So it happens that the refusal to acknowledge that life is a shared thing can actually bring about a sharing of life.

All this is complicated, and it also sounds peculiar and new, and indeed this way of thinking about life *is* new, in a way. This is the contemporary western 'way of life' which manages in a roundabout and contradictory way to express the very 'life' which it denies.

But this fact of shut-in-ness—not sharing, not really living—is not new. Nor is the experience of breaking out into a shared life, a real life. As long as there have been people on earth, they have suffered from this shut-in-ness and longed to break out and find life. Many kinds of philosophy and religion have thought of this shut-in-ness as the result of being in a body. They think of the *real* self as wanting to break free of the body, which hampers it, and prevents it experiencing its true life. Some religions have taught that the soul, the true self, will finally be freed from the body altogether, will even be freed from its own individuality, and achieve oneness with God, whom we, in our feeble imaginations and thoughts, can only conceive as 'nothing', but a 'nothing' from which all 'things' emerge and to which they return.

Christianity has often used this kind of language, and indeed the habit of talking about 'body' and 'soul' as two separate things, one shut up in the other, is so common that we often get the idea that this doctrine—the teaching that the true self is only discovered when it is freed from the body—is a Christian one. But it is not, and never was.

If you think about it carefully, you know that when you move your hand or speak there is not a separate 'something' that decides to do this, and which then causes you to do it with your body. Rather, what your body does is what *you* do. You know yourself only in doing things. Your body *is* you. What you know with your mind and feel with your hands and see with your eyes—all these are things *you* experience. Your body is *you*. All the same there are some things that *you* do, that you feel afterwards 'don't fit': they aren't what *you* really wanted to do. Yet *you* did them.

Now this curious state of affairs is what St Paul called 'the life of the flesh'. He didn't mean your body, as a separate, physical thing. He meant the life we live, a bodily life, but an unsatisfactory life in which we don't fully understand what we are or what we want, and therefore do all kinds of things that we know very well are not behaviour that belongs to what we feel we *really* are. Yet this 'life of the flesh' *is* alive, and is capable of being changed so that it can live fully—that is, enter a shared life in which we can really understand ourselves and each other, as *alive*. 'Now we see things like a confused reflection in a mirror', he says—and mirrors in his day were not nearly as clear as they are now—'but then we shall see face-to-face. Now I know *in part* but then I shall *know* as *I am known*.' It's the difference between 'living' and 'partly living'. And one can see from the way St Paul uses the word 'then' that he confidently expects this 'partly living' in the flesh to give way to a different kind of awareness that is fully 'living'.

Christianity is about how this can happen.

IV

LAW OR LIFE?

IV

LAW OR LIFE?

THE NEW TESTAMENT is a proclamation. It is an announcement of news—*good* news, in the view of the people who announce it. The word 'Gospel' means 'good news' and 'preaching the Gospel' is announcing this good news. It is an announcement that the shut-in state that St Paul calls 'life in the flesh', and which modern writers make us feel so acutely, is not the only one. There *is* real life, and *we can have it*.

So the whole Christian thing is really about life and living, yet when people discuss Christianity they usually think of it very largely in terms of rules—moral rules. Christians have a reputation for caring a lot (too much, perhaps) about rules. As I said in the second chapter, behaviour, a 'way of life', goes some way, but incompletely, unsurely, to show us what people *are*. This respect for rules is important because it has obviously played a big part in the Christian way of life through history—so much so that we naturally look for a Christian type of behaviour as the normal way of judging whether a person is Christian or not. By remarks like 'so and so is a better Christian than someone else who goes to church', we mean that so and so *behaves* in a more Christian way, in our opinion. He 'keeps the rules' that we feel Christians should keep and often don't. Yet, in a contradictory way, a person who does 'keep the rules' may seem to be *not* very Christian. By this we mean that in some way his rule-keeping is a sham, his actions are not really *his*. His way of life doesn't fit with what we feel is real *life*.

So there is this peculiar contradiction—that sometimes we feel people can properly be called 'Christian' because they behave in a Christian way, even though they don't call themselves Christian, and sometimes people behave in ways which follow Christian rules, and yet we feel their behaviour is not really Christian.

This state of affairs is one that has always worried Christians. It certainly bothered St Paul, who wrote a good deal to explain the matter to his converts. The business of keeping the rules, *behaving* according to a pattern laid down for us, is what Paul called the Law. Christ claimed to have surpassed and fulfilled the Law: St Paul said Christians are freed from the Law by Christ. In fact he said this repeatedly and emphatically —you could almost say he had an obsession about it. Yet he himself insisted on very high moral standards from his converts, and spent a lot of time describing what is Christian behaviour and what isn't. Ever since then, Christianity has given a very large—often a much too large—place to rules of behaviour, its 'way of life': the Law, in fact.

Many people have noticed this and have claimed that the Church has betrayed the message of Christ, exchanged freedom for slavery, and stifled the true life in a blanket of hypocrisy and smug do-goodery.

To a great extent this is true. If we are to see that Christianity really is about life and not just about behaviour, and yet to see how the emphasis on behaviour makes sense, provided it isn't exaggerated, and also how the exaggerations happened, then it is necessary to do a bit of fairly cautious thinking. It is easy to jump to conclusions. It is easy to say 'Christianity is about life and love, and rules don't matter', or to say 'if people behave properly they will live together happily and that is what Christianity should teach them'. Both of these ideas have a lot of truth in them, but taken alone they are neither true nor sensible, and they are contradicted by experience. In order to see this more clearly it helps to look at the development of a child and see how any human being grows up able really to live—if he does.

A baby doesn't know anything much. He can feel quite a lot, but he doesn't even know the feelings are *his*. He doesn't know there is a 'him', or that other people are people and are separate from himself. Everything around him, as well as his own body, is part of his experience. Gradually he learns what experiences are to do with himself, in his own body, and what are outside himself and outside his control. He kicks his cot, and finds that the cot is not his foot, but that he can feel the cot *with* his foot. The sensation is his, but the cot isn't himself. His mother feeds him, and for some time he doesn't distinguish between the experience of feeding and the breast that he feeds from. But then the breast is taken away, he can't get it back, he can't have the experience of feeding when he wants it—the mother who feeds him is not part of himself, after all. This is a terrifying discovery, and it only becomes bearable when he finds that, in fact, he *is* fed when he needs to be—his mother, who withdraws, also comes back, and he can rely on this. This is one (very important) example of why it matters that people should be able to rely on their surroundings—human or not—as they grow up. It is only because things and people *stay the same* that a child can learn to feel at home in himself and in his world. The bars of the cot are always solid, the same distance apart, the same colour. The mother who feeds goes away, but she comes back. Grown up people can take this sameness of things for granted; a baby can't, he has to learn it. This is why child psychologists keep on saying how important it is that one person, and not a succession of people, should care for a child, and that he should have a regular, stable routine, though of course not one so rigid that it can't be adapted to his own changing needs.

This regular and stable nature of things and people and times is part of what is meant by the Law. It makes people feel safe, and it makes it possible for them to discover *who they are*. If everything around a child constantly changes, and he is treated one minute kindly, harshly the next, is fed sometimes and not others, he has nothing to 'measure' himself against. He can't discover himself, or what he is like.

Later on the idea of Law becomes more obvious and familiar. Children need rules about their own conduct. Just as it is difficult for a child to discover who and what he is if he is treated inconsistently, so he can't discover what he wants unless he has some fixed standard by which to measure his 'wants'. If he never knows what his parents will allow or not allow, whether he is 'good' or 'naughty', he can't decide things clearly. He *daren't* make decisions, because he never knows what will happen. He may dislike being refused something he wants, but at least the refusal makes him aware that he does want it, that *he* wants it. A child who has no clear framework of rules to his life finds it very hard to judge his actions. Also this 'emptiness' of his moral world makes him feel lonely and cut off. Nobody seems to care what he does, his actions don't seem to 'touch' anybody, or bring him into relation with anyone. He would very much prefer to be spanked than ignored, which is why children who feel neglected often try to provoke their parents to anger. At least, if your mother slaps you, you can be sure she knows you are *there*.

This framework of unchanging facts and consistent rules of behaviour is all part of the idea of Law. Obviously, we need this in order to grow up at all. The insecure child is unable to discover, afraid to try new things, unwilling to trust. The secure child can dare to take risks, to adventure, to reach out to new experiences.

But this framework is only a framework. In a sense, it is 'outside' us, although we experience it and so it is also 'inside' us. But it isn't *ours*. It is made for us by powers outside ourselves. Growing up doesn't mean discarding all this framework—life would be impossible without this continuity in things and customs and laws, though they can and must change and adapt to new needs and ideas. But growing up properly does mean learning to decide for oneself, learning to *use* the framework of the Law, rather than simply obeying because that is the usual thing.

Children find this out gradually, partly by disobeying. They discover that they don't *have* to obey, but once that is clear they also discover that there are reasons why the order was given, the custom established. The Law is no longer just 'I tell you'—it becomes clear that in many cases this or that bit of Law is something *I* need, myself. Then, if I obey, I do so freely, by my own decision. This doesn't mean that we need always fully understand the reasons why things are arranged as they are. If we have good reason to believe that the framework is a good one, we shall be prepared to obey —freely—even if parts of it seem incomprehensible, or even if we dislike it intensely. (Like paying taxes, for instance.) On the other hand if we begin to think that part of the framework, the Law, is *not* really helping people to grow up and discover themselves but is restricting them, then we question it and try to get it altered.

This we can do because we are free. And we are still free when we obey because we decide to.

Now all this growing up happens 'according to the Law', in St Paul's sense. All this behaviour is the behaviour of people who live, as we all do, 'in the flesh', but we *regulate* that life by the Law, so that we can live peacefully, and grow up and discover ourselves.

Yet this self-discovery, which is the discovery of real living, is not something the Law can do for us. No amount of obeying rules—even the grown-up, free obedience—can give the experience of life. All it can do is to organize our way of life so that we can have the opportunity to experience life—and *also be able to take the opportunity when it comes.* But this 'all' is absolutely essential. The kind of bringing up that a person gets 'according to the Law' decides what kind of person he will be, it makes it possible or *im*possible for him to come to a full experience of life—one that can grow, and change his *whole* life.

This is the reason why Christianity has always been concerned about Law. It has to be. If people live by a framework which is too harsh, or not secure enough, or which contains rules that are *against* life, then they won't be 'formed' so that they are able to live fully. For instance, a framework of life that takes slavery for granted makes the slaves' lives less than human, because they are deprived of the power of decision. They cannot make lasting relationships, for at any moment they may be sent away. This makes people bitter and selfish, and the only experience of liveness they can hope for is the quick, furtive pleasure of sex or of cruelty, or the escape of a phantasy life. And slavery affects the slave-owners also. They become used to treating other human beings as less than human. Their own ability to love is stunted. This is only one example of how a framework of living may be enduring and work well and yet be wrong, from the point of view of the power to live fully. There are all too many examples of the same thing, in societies in which there are obvious injustices. I don't mean only frightful things in the past, like child labour in mines and factories, but things we are quite used to now, like the fact that some families have decent houses and gardens while others are crowded with eight or ten people to a room, with no proper sanitation and nowhere for children to play. People who are able to know that this goes on, and not mind, are people whose minds have been to some extent stunted and 'toughened'. This means they will find it harder to accept the full experience of life. They will find it harder in proportion as they have denied it to others—not by actually ill-treating people, but by feeling that what is happening to these other human beings doesn't matter.

It is the kind of upbringing people have—the kind of framework they live in—that fixes to a great extent (not altogether) how people react when they come up against the opportunities of life. This is why a proper *formation* for living is necessary, as well as the *opportunities* for it. This formation is the business of Law in the Christian sense, and so Christianity is bound to be very much concerned with rules and customs, with behaviour in general

—in fact with Law—not because Christianity is about the Law, but because without the Law there can be no discovery of the real life that is much more important than any Law.

In practice, as everyone knows, this Christian care for Law has often become so important that nothing else seemed to matter. And besides, Christians have often become used to the framework in which they happen to have been born, and have not noticed that it imposed un-Christian behaviour. Christians have often obeyed and even imposed unjust laws, and accepted unjust social conditions and immoral ideas. In doing this they were actually betraying their Christianity, and contradicting the purpose of the Church's existence. If, in spite of all this, we want to maintain that Christianity *is* about life and is true, then we must not pretend that the past and present crimes of Christians don't matter. They do matter, and we can't ignore them. Why is it that the Law, which should help people to live, has so often been deadly? Why is it that the Church, which should help people to grow up to live, by a Law designed for this purpose, so often restricts people, seems to deaden rather than make alive? Why should we imagine that a huge and unwieldly human organization like the Church could bring us the good news of life? Isn't the Church a matter of Law, rules, ancient habits? Isn't life a spontaneous thing that grows between people meeting and loving?

To go back to what I said in Chapter III, is Christianity concerned with living, or only with 'partly living'? Another question also arises—if the Church (any Church) is so often heavy-handed and obsessed with Law, wouldn't Christianity be better off without it? Couldn't the proclamation of the good news be done better without this hampering framework of rules and customs?

V

HOW ODD OF GOD—

V

HOW ODD OF GOD—

THE LAST CHAPTER raised some fundamental questions about what Christianity is really like, and also what the Church is, in relation to Christianity.

In order to answer them we have now to look at the subject in quite a different way. So far I have discussed the ideas of 'life' and 'realness' as experiences that we can all recognize in our personal lives, and I have also discussed how the Law is necessary to the discovery of life. Now I want to leave the personal angle and examine the same idea—but historically.

Christianity began with Christ, but in a sense Christ didn't begin Christianity. The ideas and attitudes and hopes that helped to make up the pattern of Christian thought have their roots much further back than that.

They grew—because Jesus Christ did—out of the experiences of one very peculiar nation, the people called the Jews.

'How odd
of God
to choose
the Jews,'

wrote Hilaire Belloc, who didn't much like them. And in a way, it *is* odd that the founder of a movement that changed the course of history (and introduced into the world a totally new concept of what human life is about) should have sprung from an obscure little nation, one of the many subject peoples of Rome, and a backward one at that, with no great degree of civilization and no artistic achievements to its credit except a collection of sacred writings—which no one else considered important, anyway. Even at the height of its brief prosperity, under King Solomon, the kingdom of Israel could never compete in power or achievement with the great civilizations of the past—Egypt, Crete, Persia, India, China, Greece. In fact what it did achieve was mostly copied from surrounding nations. Its previous history was that of a tiny but warlike people who won their country by invading it and ruthlessly blotting out the people already living there. Having won it they were incessantly engaged in fighting and feuding among themselves, whenever they weren't fully occupied in fending off enemies. After Solomon the story becomes more and more sordid and depressing—rivalries, civil war, assassination, repression, revenge, plots, broken treaties and dubious political machinations, all ending in the total destruction of the capital city and the enslavement and deportation of the remnants of the population. Eventually they came back and rebuilt Jerusalem, but their comparative independence was short-lived. Before long they were under the domination of foreign powers once more, first Greek and then Roman. But they were so impervious to civilization, so obstinately rebellious and troublesome, that even the tolerant Romans got tired in the end. In A.D. 70 the nation as a nation was finally wiped out after a war (of whose atrocities we are learning more through recent excavations at Masada) culminating in the seige of Jerusalem, the most horrible seige in all history. The people were scattered, and did not return until the new state of Israel was established after the last war. With that sort of record, how odd, indeed, to choose the Jews.

But from another point of view Belloc's witty little verse simply shows ignorance of the subject. To speak in that way is to talk as if God decided he had to do something about the mess the world was in, looked around for a likely nation for his purposes, and picked the Jews. This makes it sound silly—and it *is* silly, however you dress it up in earnest language to make it seem serious. If one can really think of God like that then this isn't a God one could take seriously, certainly not the God who is known in Jesus Christ.

Because the whole point about the Jews is that they *were* chosen. It was their sense of being chosen that made them different from other nations. From the very beginning of their history—as soon as they knew they *had* a history—they told it as the story of this choosing.

When they looked back, and told the story of Abraham their forefather, they did not tell it as the tale of some hero, like the Greek or Egyptian myth heroes of antiquity, who by his great deeds won power for his people. They told it as the story of a man called by God, whose life was directed by this calling. All his failures are failures to trust in this calling, his successes come from obedience to it. It is the same with his sons and grandsons. Jacob, his grandson, appears as a commercially minded and not very honest adventurer, while his twin, Esau, is an honest, rugged character whom one can't help liking. But Esau is disgraced because he does not realize the importance of his calling. Jacob, the supplanter, receives the blessing because he values that calling, and is prepared to follow it, according to his (rather dubious) lights.

But these were stories the Jews told each other much later, and the angle from which they told them was established because by that time they had realized themselves—the whole nation—as chosen. They often spoke of the nation as if it were one person—Israel, which was Jacob's other name. It was as if Israel, the man, contained in his own person the whole nation, and the nation saw in the calling of the man, Israel, the symbol of its own calling.

But the experience that made Israel a nation, and gave it this tremendous sense of vocation, was something that happened long after the calling of Abraham, Isaac and Jacob. What marked the consciousness of the nation forever was the traumatic experience of the long captivity in Egypt, and the break to freedom that ended it.

Moses, the saviour of his people, was the man whose terrific personality and fiery faith has come through the mists of myth and legend, and can still impress us with the sense of a vividly real man, even when the details of his historical career are impossible to establish with accuracy. He defied the rulers, but that was easy compared with the task of giving a down-trodden people sufficient faith in themselves to attempt the break to freedom. If people are treated as sub-human they get to *feel* sub-human, and accept their condition. They may cease to want any other, even though they resent it and suffer under it. This has been happening in South Africa, where Africans get used to thinking of themselves as slightly despicable, untrustworthy, though perhaps pleasant and amusing, creatures—because that is how they are treated. The very words in which they talk about themselves are words *meaning* inferior, not fully human, people. Since there are no other words to use, Africans as well as Whites get to feel that Africans *are* like this. Similarly, people in mental hospitals are treated as irresponsible, the things they say are *assumed* to be nonsense. So as well as the burden of their unusual experiences, which separate them from others, they have to struggle against the feeling that their efforts to get in touch again are useless, that they aren't *capable* of being or saying anything meaningful.

This was the sort of thing that happened to the children of Israel. They were used to being slaves, and although they were often ill-treated they were safe, their food and shelter was assured, provided they did what they were told. They could even hope to be accepted into Egyptian society, in some cases, if they were clever and adaptable, and prepared to accept all the customs and values of Egypt. This was what happened to Moses, apparently (unless, as some have suggested, he was actually an Egyptian—but this seems unlikely). But Moses got into trouble with the authorities, fled the country, and spent some time among the tribes of the desert. It was in this solitude—away from the Egyptian influence that made Hebrews feel inferior—that he realized himself as a man with a mission and became aware of a power acting in him that was greater than Egyptian culture and politics.

He managed to convey this to the depressed Hebrew slaves, though it took some doing, and every time there was a setback they lost their nerve and cursed him for upsetting things.

In the end a number of them broke out and managed to get clear of the country altogether. This was a huge achievement in itself—it is characteristic of slaves that, since they are treated as irresponsible, they are timid and lack initiative. (This fact is often given nowadays as a reason for not giving subject peoples their freedom.) Therefore it was vital—and difficult—to work them up to the point of deciding to go. It was the conviction Moses managed to pump into them, that God cared for them and was 'on their side', that persuaded them to take the huge risk. For it was a horrible risk they took.

They knew all too well the kind of thing that happened to escaped slaves who were re-captured. (The civilized Egyptians were experts in judicial torture.)

But, having got them out, Moses knew that something more than the temporary exhilaration of freedom was needed in order to get them through the hard years ahead, when they would have to fight for every inch of the country to which he was leading them.

The period that the Hebrews spent in the desert was immensely important for them. They looked back on it as a golden age, when their forefathers lived on God's bounty from day to day, obeyed his will, and were not distracted by the luxury and pride of the great civilized nations with their 'strange gods'. The later prophets were always reminding their people of this early time when God chose a poor, powerless rabble of ex-slaves and made them into one people, founded in faith and strong in their calling. And the thing that drew the people together and formed them as the Chosen of the Lord was the Law. Moses was the Law-giver. Later generations elaborated and explained the Law, but it was always called 'the Law of Moses', because the giving of the Law was an immensely important part of Moses' work as saviour.

The Law was the sign that the Hebrews were a *chosen* people. Because of it they were different, called out from among the nations for a special task. It was not a law like that of other nations, though in fact many of the rules were derived from the codes of Egyptian wisdom and of Hammurabi. But the Hebrews thought of the Law as *God's* Law, even the most practical details of it. These rules of daily life and observance—these routines of 'partly living'—were all seen as part of their vocation as God's people. Because God had chosen them, they were 'a holy people, a consecrated nation', and everything they did and felt and hoped was therefore part of this new life to which God had called them when he set them free.

'Hear, O Israel,' the book of Deuteronomy cried to them centuries later, reminding them of their destiny in a prayer that has been and is still recited daily by Jews—'Hear, O Israel! The Lord our God, the Lord is one!' God was not a national, limited God, fighting with other gods and perhaps winning. God was one, supreme, unimaginable, other, wholly beyond the power of man to control or describe. But he had chosen Israel for his own.

> 'For you are a people made holy to the Lord your God', the prayer goes on. 'The Lord your God has chosen you to be his own people out of all the nations on the earth. It was not because you were more in number than any other people that the Lord set his heart upon you and chose you, for you are the least of all peoples. But it is because the Lord loves you, and is keeping the promise that he made to your forefathers, that the Lord has brought you out with a strong hand and saved you from the house of bondage, and from the hand of Pharaoh King of Egypt. Know therefore that the Lord your God *is* God, the

faithful God who keeps covenant and steadfast love with those who love him and keep his commandments, from generation to generation.'

The Law—the 'commandments'—were the sign that the people was a chosen, holy people. And the 'covenant' was the way the Hebrews expressed their sense of being God's chosen. The covenant was a promise and an invitation. A promise of God's care and love and an invitation to respond to that love by loving in return. And the way to show that the invitation was accepted, the love returned, the promise realized, was to 'keep the commandments'. The commandments were the sign of being the people of the covenant.

Later on, Israel's prophets compared the relationship of God and Israel to the love between man and wife. It is a relationship of covenant—a response to an invitation to love, and this response is made in the exchange of promises. And the way Israel is to carry out her part of the promise is by obedience to the Law, which is the sign of her calling, which makes her holy. It is a response of love, for Israel is the bride of the Lord, not his slave.

It is a wonderful idea. You can see how, at its best, this vision of a people called to share intimately in the life and purpose of their creator could inspire all its members, and give meaning to their lives. It made them able to overcome enemies stronger and more civilized than themselves, because they fought with the energy and conviction of faith. They were savage, they were superstitious, they were cruel, but they really were living by a vision that was utterly different from any idea of life that the surrounding nations had.

In practice, of course, it was hard to keep this pure faith and hope alive. The history of Israel is a long story of failure to live up to this calling. They imitated other nations, they adopted their gods (who were less interfering than the Lord), they played at politics. In the end they did grow powerful for a while, but at the expense of faith. And it didn't last. Israel degenerated rapidly, as I described earlier.

But it was precisely during this period of degeneration, when Israel was divided and finally conquered, that there arose the great prophets, whose writings show us, as the 'history' books of the Old Testament could not do, what the people of Israel is really *about*. In a sense, the things Isaiah and Jeremiah told their people to do were impossible. They demanded that Israel should stop trying to win safety by treaties or power of arms, but seek safety only in the Lord, by obeying him and leaving the future to him. Politics and war are not for you, they said, you are not called for this—your destiny is greater than that, you are called to be a holy people, so that the knowledge of the Lord may spread to other nations, and 'the nations shall walk in the brightness of thy rising'. Death and destruction will come, they said, because Israel has been an unfaithful wife to the Lord. But a few, a faithful remnant, will go on, and begin again.

And gradually another idea began to emerge in the

minds of the people of Israel, and the prophets proclaimed it. God has made a covenant with us, he cannot fail, *somehow* it will come true. The covenant we know has not worked, we have not become holy—if God's promise is to be fulfilled there must be a *new* covenant, growing out of the old one and cancelling it.

Then, through the remaining centuries, images and prayers grew together around this hope, and the prophets saw, as the instrument of God to fulfil his promise, the figure of a man. Was he Israel in person? Was he a warrior king who would give freedom—like Cyrus, the Persian, who sent the Jews back to their ruined city and allowed them to rebuild it? Or was he a kind of Angel—a Messenger of God's power to men? Was he another David, to unify his people and free them from oppression? Or was he a prophet, to strike terror, and to heal?

During the years that followed the return of the Jews to Jerusalem, when they were a subject nation, resentful and powerless, this hope grew and grew. One day, they were sure, the Anointed of God would come. Then Israel would be free. Perhaps it would be the end of the world and the beginning of a new world. Perhaps the Day of the Lord would end sorrow and pain forever, and the chosen of God would live at peace, in a world where even wild animals were gentle. 'The lion shall lie down with the lamb, and a little child shall lead them.'

Meanwhile, the Roman Empire grew, became solid and assured. The best roads ever built spread out across many nations, carrying news quickly. The world of the

Empire was at peace, ships came and went in safety. Trade and travel flourished. All nations had a common language—the rough but useful *koine* Greek. Never before had there been such a stable peace and such ease of communication. And in the obscure but troublesome province of Judea, a boy was born to a respectable peasant couple. His name was Yeshua-bar-Yoseph. We call him Jesus Christ.

VI

PREACHING THE GOOD NEWS—WHAT GOOD NEWS?

VI

PREACHING THE GOOD NEWS—WHAT GOOD NEWS?

BY THE TIME Jesus of Nazareth was born, the Law of Moses, which was meant to be the love-offering of Israel to her husband, didn't feel like that to the Jews. Just as devoted parents sometimes go on treating their teen-agers like ten year olds, because they are afraid for them, so the leaders of the Jews were using the Law as a protection for the people. By making the rules absolutely fool-proof, it seemed to be unnecessary for people to worry about their conduct. They simply had to obey the rules, and this would *protect* them from the influence of the surrounding paganism. God's people had to be separate, cut off, 'a garden enclosed'. But whereas the prophets had seen this separation as the means to form a people for a great mission, the new leaders saw it as an end in itself. Mixing with foreigners (Gentiles) was *the* sin, and the Law—elaborated in endless detailed rulings by trained lawyers—was the way to avoid this.

So the Law, the sign of God's love and calling, the pledge of a free people, became a kind of slavery. It was a burden too heavy for ordinary people to carry, though specially fervent (usually well-to-do) Jews made it their life's work to carry out the Law down to the last detail. These were the Pharisees. They had once been the agents of reform, prophets in their way, reminding a nation too much influenced by pagan philosophy and art that Israel was a chosen people, called and sealed, and the sign of this was the Law.

But so often reformers end up by being more rigid than the ideas they have tried to reform. The Pharisees ended by seeing the Law no longer as a sign of a greater reality—the 'way of life' of God's people with their God—but as sufficient in itself. They behaved and taught as if the Law itself were the way to be 'right' with God. 'Partly living' was enough, provided it was law-abiding.

Yet even Moses had never taught that. The Law was not *why* the people were chosen; it was the means they used in order to become worthy of being chosen. And when there came a man who said he was 'greater than Moses' this was exactly what he kept on telling the people. From that moment, it was war to the death between him and the lawyers and Pharisees.

The real holiness is a new and different kind of life, he said. The message of Jesus of Nazareth is about this life. 'I have not come to destroy the Law, but to fulfil it,' he told his critics, but that didn't reassure them. To them, the Law was the way of holiness itself. To him, Law was a way to help people to realize holiness, but holiness could not be attained by obeying the Law. Obviously, to get any idea of what Christianity is, and why one should be a Christian, it is essential to have a clear idea of what was this message, the Christian 'Gospel', which Jesus' followers preached. Growing out of Judaism, with its emphasis on Law, came this call to look 'through' the Law and find and seize on life. How? He offered 'life' and claimed to be able to *give* it. How can we get at what he meant, and what it means to us?

Because Jesus lived and died and rose again before the apostles went out to spread his 'good news', and also because in the Bible the Gospels and Acts are printed before the Epistles, we are apt to think of the Gospels as being somehow 'nearer' to the message of Jesus, more 'original', more authentic. We think of the Epistles as explaining and perhaps adding to Gospel teaching. They seem a rather abstract (and boring?) follow-up to the directness and simplicity of the Gospel message. Many people have even said, and still do say, that St Paul was distorting and complicating the original purity of the Gospel. Indeed, the Gospels *are* much easier to read, and we naturally feel that because we can easily understand the narrative style (at least of the first three Gospels) it is all quite straightforward, and we can do without the complexities of Paul.

But, historically, the thing is not so simple. For one

thing, the Epistles were written before the Gospels. And the Epistles were meant to clear up muddles and explain difficulties which had arisen in the business of building of the first Christian communities. The communities grew up in response to the preaching of 'the Gospel'—the good news. So the *original* Gospel is something that, in one sense, we can't get at at all. The very first Christians were so convinced of the newness of the life they had received that it seemed ridiculous to suppose that the old, sin-distorted, groping, 'partly living' world could go on much longer. They expected the return of Christ and the final triumph of God's kingdom any minute. What we call 'the Gospels' are books written at a time when it was becoming clear that the world was unlikely to come to an end this year or next. In that case, the preaching of the Gospel must go on. But the twelve, and Paul—the original preachers—were getting on in years. Also, they couldn't be everywhere at once, to remember and explain the teaching of Jesus and the importance of his life and death and resurrection. So the preaching must also be put into a form that could be read and discussed and handed on. But it was still *preaching*. It was still a proclamation, not a story, still less a biography.

The four Gospels were written at different times, for different kinds of communities who had different worries and doubts and used different kinds of ideas in thinking about life. So there are immense differences in the kind of proclamation that goes on in each book. The time and place of writing and the readership and writers of each is a fascinating subject, but it would be murdering it to squeeze the discussion of it into this small space. It is enough to say here that Luke, who was a 'Gentile' and acquainted with Greek historians and their methods, was by far the most 'biographical' of the four, and checked his facts carefully with eye-witnesses. But even he does not write a biography: he uses accumulated biographical detail very freely to build up a picture of Jesus, but the point of this is to give power and 'punch' to the message of salvation which he is proclaiming—salvation for all, not just Jews. The material is used to *preach the Gospel*, and every bit is chosen and arranged with this aim in mind. Matthew and Mark are even less concerned with biography, they simply want to preach, and every story and saying is presented in such a way as to make the greatest impression for this purpose. John—the last and the oddest—seems to choose the incidents of Jesus' life in order to let them show, in the 'language' of action, what he is also saying in words about the meaning of the coming of Christ.

In other words the Gospels are not at all straightforward, they are a very sophisticated and special form of literature, written with one purpose in mind and one only: the creating of faith in Jesus Christ. The people who heard them read were mostly already Christians. The Gospels confirmed and increased their faith, giving them a new experience of the life into which they had entered. They *already knew* that they 'lived', and were set free, and it was in the light of this knowledge that they heard the Gospels and were able to understand the message they contained.

If *we* want to realize the message of the Gospels we have to read them in this light, also. This does not mean that it is useless to read the Gospels unless you are already a convinced Christian. (Many people have been converted by reading them. The impact of the personality of Jesus, even through the veil of a literary form which is strange and baffling to us, is so tremendous that it moves people now as it did when he walked in Judæa and Galilee. They can and do respond to him.) It does mean that if you are to get the full impact of what the Gospels are proclaiming you have to know the kind of thing they were trying to do, which was exactly what was already being done by word of mouth and by letter. The word of mouth preaching we can't get at directly, but we can get a good idea of it from the letters that were written to supplement it and sort out difficulties. It is important to try to do this, not just as a kind of historical guessing-game, but because the way it all grew gives a clue to what was going on—the same thing that has to go on, now, if anyone is to accept the Christian message.

What went on was very odd indeed. Wherever the apostles went little groups of believers grew up, and the groups grew in members and in number. By the end of the first century the Roman Empire was riddled with them, and they appeared to be a serious menace to the State. They had already suffered fierce persecution, were well organized, 'traditional' and still growing fast. Why did this happen? What was it about the message that aroused so much faith and so much hostility?

One common explanation is that the message of Jesus spread so fast and especially among the poor, because it offered the hope of a life after death to compensate for the miseries of earthly life. It also gave down-trodden people the feeling of being actually more blessed than those who oppressed them. A more sophisticated (and much more historically credible) version of this is the suggestion that Christianity offered the sense of sharing in a secret, inner world, vastly more significant than the huge impersonal life of the city and the Empire. It was the sense of being 'initiates', people with special gifts and knowledge, that worked so powerfully. This would make the group who were admitted to the secrets of God feel able to ignore the miseries and frustrations of life. According to this view, Christianity was in this respect one more of the many 'mystery' religions that initiated people by slow and often painful and absolutely secret stages and ceremonies into the full knowledge of the god. This full knowledge was salvation, freedom from the rules and burdens of earthly life, even from the concern of the body, which was evil. Some held that the fully initiated were so liberated from human rules that they could do as they liked with their bodies, which did not affect the 'spiritual' part of the truly spiritual man. Others, on the contrary, ill-treated their bodies in order to secure greater liberty for the spirit. But the principle was the same—the body was evil, the soul was the only part of man capable of salvation. There were many versions of such ideas.

This account of early Christianity clearly does not fit in with the kind of teaching found in the four Gospels, with its emphasis on practical charity. But suppose the early teaching had quickly been accommodated to the needs of the foreign cities, where the mystery cults flourished? (They did flourish for the reasons suggested in the last paragraph.) St Paul is often blamed for doing just this and, in his letter to Colossae and to the Gentile Churches (Ephesians) especially, he uses the language of these teachings, he talks of the kingdom of 'Light' and of 'Darkness'—which these teachings thought of as equal and warring powers. He talks of 'mysteries', of 'powers'—spiritual beings whose work was to liberate the divine spark of light in man from the surrounding darkness of the evil, fleshly world.

Besides this kind of language in Paul's letters, there is the fact that teaching of this kind did become very influential among Christians, and that there have been, ever since, Christians who did interpret their beliefs along these lines. 'Gnostic' teaching—the notion that only those who have special, secret 'knowledge' (*gnosis*) can be saved—is always popular, today as much as ever. The cult of LSD is one example of the same craving for enlightenment. Another is the popularity of oriental religions that work for final liberation from the body. More crudely, horoscopes and spiritualism promise a way of discovering the ultimate truth through special knowledge.

I am not concerned to discuss the value of these ideas here, but to ask whether it was this sort of thing that made Christianity so influential and so 'catching' in the first century.

There are certain undoubted facts that tell forcibly against it.

One is that those letters of Paul which use this sort of language are actually directed *against* these teachings. He used this kind of language because he knew his readers would understand it—but he used the words in a way that gave an entirely new twist to them. Believe in powers and mysteries if you like, he is saying, and in the battle of light and darkness, but do realize that there is only *one* power that really matters—the power of Christ's resurrection, the power of a life that you can share; there is a great 'mystery', but it's a mystery of *love*—love of Christ in *people*: bodily, ordinary people. The kingdom of light is Christ's kingdom, whose light is love, and that love involves the whole of life, not just 'knowledge'. If there is darkness it is the darkness of sin, and you are freed from it by the power of the love of Christ.

The other fact is that the mystery religions and gnostic teachings were for the select few. It is true that the devotees tried to attract others, but selectively, and of those who accepted these teachings only a few were able to become full initiates. The cults spread, but always under cover: they were essentially secret and mysterious. They were never preached in public. But the whole point about the Christian good news was that it was news for 'all nations', for everybody, and for all equally. 'There is neither Jew nor Greek, there is neither slave nor free, there is neither male nor female; for you are all one in Christ Jesus,' wrote Paul to the Galatians, who were worried by teachers who said that *proper* Christians should keep the Law of Moses. It isn't the Law that makes you holy, Paul kept on saying, it is faith in Christ. 'Are you mad, Galatians?' he wrote—because they were giving up their new-found freedom and looking to the Law for salvation. Not 'knowledge' or 'mysteries' or 'the Law', or anything else on earth can help men to discover the real life, but only faith in Christ, risen and glorified.

This was the original message, this was the good news. 'It is the power of God to save all who have faith,' he wrote to the Roman Church, and he summed up the whole thing in a sentence in that same letter:

> 'Both Jew and pagan have sinned and are without God's presence, but both are justified by a freely given grace, by being redeemed in Christ Jesus, who was appointed by God to sacrifice his life so as to win reconciliation through faith.'

This was the message that changed the world. But to anyone who has had a Christian education of even the sketchiest kind—or even been to church a few times—these words are extremely familiar, and not at all exciting. They can even be rather repulsive, they sound like magic, a sort of game by which God deprives people of life, then gives it back—not because they deserve it but because Jesus 'makes up for' their sins (which they couldn't help, anyway, having been born like that). And all the business about sacrifice—why should God want a *death*, like the old pagan gods? And faith—it usually seems to mean believing what you are told without thinking about it too much.

A well-educated Christian doesn't have this crude idea of what Paul is talking about (though that is what a lot of non-Christians think that Christians really believe) but even if you know fairly well what Paul was getting at, does it seem to be something you *know* in your own personal life? If you heard this teaching for the first time, would you find it exciting? So extra-ordinary that it changed your life? So glorious that you couldn't rest until you told everyone you knew? The answer is, probably, 'no'.

But it had that effect on the people who heard it. And they were quite ordinary people. In that case, presumably they understood this preaching in a way in which we don't, usually. It 'rang a bell'. It was like a lightning flash, illuminating their whole lives.

What Paul, and the others, preached was 'as of first importance, what I also received, that Christ died for our sins in accordance with the scriptures, that he was buried, that he was raised on the third day . . . so we preached and so you believed.' What does it really mean? How can *this* bring people out of 'partly living' into full living?

VII

'WE SAW HIS GLORY—'

VII

'WE SAW HIS GLORY—'

IT HELPS US to see what the all-too-familiar Christian statements mean, and why they made such a stir, if we realize that the people who preached the good news—Paul and the others—took as their starting point something people *knew*. They referred to a need their hearers *recognized*.

Nowadays, we sometimes get the impression that Christian teachers and preachers are saying, basically, 'you may not want what we are offering, but you *ought* to, it's good for you,' like a mother trying to persuade a child to eat spinach, 'because it'll make you strong'.

But Christian preaching is effective when people realize it is talking about a need and a longing that they realize. To try and make people feel guilty, so that they *then* want forgiveness and look for it in religion, is not uncommon as a method of trying to 'convert' people, but it can never lead to a true conversion. Conversion is an opening out, an act of love, whereas running to the church or to God for protection from one's own sins is an act of fear, a shutting-out of danger, a shutting-in for the sake of security.

The first Christians were converted because they knew they lacked something, and realized that they were being offered it. This lack was the same sort of lack that I said in an earlier chapter made one family less attractive than another. It was a lack of liveness and realness in their lives. It was the sense of dreary pointlessness that haunts people today, also. It was the restless and yet almost hopeless desire for something 'behind' or 'inside' or 'above' (choose your metaphor, it makes no difference) the necessary routines of partly living. It was the kind of feeling of discontent and longing that made people take to the mystery religions in order to find a meaning in life, and that still drives people to the same kind of pursuits. It was the stifling feeling of helplessness to alter things—even to alter oneself—combined with the maddening conviction that one *should* be able to alter things, including oneself.

This was the condition Paul referred to as 'being in the flesh' or 'being in our sins'. Although people are born to a life that just is like this, and therefore can't help it, this kind of life does make people ill-treat and hate and distrust each other and even themselves—in other words it leads to *sin*. This is why we can talk of this state of affairs as sinful, or being 'in sin', even though people are not fully responsible for all the wrong they do and suffer. Those first preachers used these words and phrases because the people they were talking to were accustomed to them, and knew what they meant—they knew the words were about something they really experienced. So the preaching 'rang a bell' as clearly as if, for instance, you were in prison and someone told you you could be set free. If you were told this, you wouldn't wonder what he meant or whether it mattered. You would know. The word 'prison' would mean a condition you knew and disliked, and 'freedom' would mean getting *out* of it. You would not be in any doubt about whether getting out was desirable.

But if you had been in prison so long that you could neither remember nor imagine any other life, the message might seem meaningless. (This can happen to people imprisoned or enslaved for very long periods.) In that case you might well be extremely suspicious and angry at this attempt to make you leave the only life you knew. After all, prison is safe, you can get along quite well if you know the rules and keep on the right side of the warders—who are quite pleasant chaps once you get to know them.

This comparison gives a good idea of why some people flocked round the apostles, demanding to be baptized, while others were so angry at their preaching that they did their best to get them imprisoned and killed.

It is interesting to notice, also, the kind of people who responded to the message. They were, generally speaking (there were brilliant exceptions) not well-to-do people, not the ruling classes or the respectable. Christ once told a group of influential Jews that the tax-collectors (whom they despised as servants of Rome and traitors to their own people) and prostitutes would go into the kingdom of heaven ahead of the law-abiding. And it was true—it was the weak and sick and sinful that followed him. When his followers went out to preach it was, again, mainly the poor and downtrodden who listened. The opposition came normally from the prosperous and virtuous citizens.

Our 'prison' comparison throws light on why this was so. The well-to-do and respected were people who had managed to make themselves *comfortable* in the shut-in 'life of the flesh'. By organizing it well, and assuring themselves that they had all that mattered, they had come to feel little need for anything else. If odd desires did stir under the surface, they could be stifled without much difficulty, because to let them become important would endanger the things one had which were clearly *good*—home and comfort and friends and the satisfaction of doing right and being respected. The tragic story of the 'rich young man' shows this clearly. He came to Jesus because he genuinely admired him and wanted to follow him. But when it came to the point he could not accept the idea that all the good things he had were unimportant by comparison with the new life of the 'kingdom' he was being offered. So he 'went away sorrowful'.

But those who listened to the message of freedom, and rose up with joy to enter that freedom, were those whose lives had made them realize acutely their state of 'imprisonment'. They were not cushioned against the knowledge by comfort and respectability. They *knew* they were sinners—in the sense I described above. It wasn't just a question of being sorry for wrong done as if the sin were a sort of 'stain' or 'growth' that could be scrubbed off. Sin, like all kinds of behaviour, is *oneself*. When people were converted, and asked for baptism, they didn't think they were discarding an unpleasant 'extra', so that they could be better people. They knew it meant changing *themselves*, entering a new kind of existence, in which the life of sin no longer ruled and conditioned everything. And ever since then it has been the people whose lives have forced them to realize fully the unsatisfying nature of human existence as we normally live it who have responded to the preaching of the good news.

So the first Christian converts recognized what the messengers of Christ meant about sin and about freedom—the freedom of a new and real life. They also recognized that what they were being offered really was the way to freedom. What made them so sure? To return to the 'prison' image: if a man had been in prison a long time and had forgotten what the outside world was like, he might indeed *want* freedom, but he might wonder whether it was really possible—if there were an outside world at all. And possibly the warders might have teased him with promises of freedom, when all they meant was extra privileges, or a chance to work in the governor's garden for a while. So, when the message of freedom was brought, he might wonder whether it was genuine. He would want to be sure the messenger was trustworthy. It wouldn't be enough if the messenger were a fellow-prisoner. He might be perfectly truthful, a good friend, yet he might be wrong—how could *he* be sure there really was a free world outside? The messenger must be someone who has been 'out' himself, who knows, from personal experience, that there is a world outside. He must be able to bear witness to the reality of the life of freedom, and also—because prisoners grow timid and distrustful—he must be able to convince the prisoner that he really cares for him and would not cheat him with false hopes.

There is another difficulty, too. Even supposing this messenger himself comes from the free life outside, is it certain that the prisoner can follow him? Will 'they' let him go? Even though the prisoner is convinced that there *is* freedom, he might well wonder whether he could reach it. But if the messenger was able to say 'I've been a prisoner myself, I know all about it—but I broke free. There *is* a way, I've made an escape route, and you can use it', then the thing begins to look different.

There is one further doubt, however, that might plague the prisoner who longs for freedom. He might say, 'This outside world—I believe it's there, I believe I *can* get out, but how safe shall I be? May not the powerful people who made this prison recapture me? You, the messenger, did escape, but how can you be sure it isn't all a trap?' But this messenger can say, 'I can guide you to a true and lasting freedom because I *know* the free world, I belong there. I live in it as my natural "kingdom". I have been a prisoner, but not because I had committed any crime, not because prison was my normal condition, but solely because I *wanted* to be there in order to make it possible for the prisoners to escape. I knew they would never believe me unless I had been a prisoner too. I made a way out, with great labour and pain, and you can use it—but you must trust me absolutely. The way out is a nasty, cold dark hole in the foundations of the prison, and no one in their senses would go into it unless they knew for certain it was the only way to the life of freedom. But you can trust me. I came from the life of freedom, and I broke out to it again in agony and loneliness. Why should I do that except for love of you? And if I did so much for love, surely that shows you can trust me.'

This image gives a clear, though obviously inadequate, idea of the kind of message that the apostles tried to put over. The message was that the man, Jesus Christ, not only had life in him but in a sense *was* himself the life, and he offered a way to the achievement of full life. But also he was himself that way, for it was by trusting him, believing in the truth of his words because he *is* truth, that others could achieve freedom and life with him and in him. And they should believe in him because his love was evident—he suffered, he died an agonizing and shameful death, not because he had to but purely because this was the only way to freedom for himself and mankind.

The word 'sacrifice' was used to describe this voluntary death, because all those who heard it knew what it meant. It meant that something to do with purely human life (animals or food) was given to God and thereby changed, in some way 'made holy' so that it became a divine thing, not merely a human thing.

This was the idea behind the pagan and the Jewish sacrifices. They were a sign that people wanted to be linked by this means to the 'real' life of the god. And Christ, said his messengers, entered into the reality of life by this kind of 'change-over', giving himself and being 'made holy', which is what 'sacrificed' means. But since it was his *own* life it wasn't just a sign of human desire for life, it was the real thing, a real breakthrough that could let others out. It could change *them* from 'partly living'—what Paul called 'death' because death was its permanent condition and meaning as well as its obvious end—to life.

But there was one very important part of this preaching which is often overlooked. It did not promise liberation in the future, at the end of life or after a long process of purification. The whole point was, as Paul kept on saying, 'the day of salvation is *now*!' 'The kingdom of heaven is *here*' the first disciples proclaimed, in the words of the first two Gospel writers who were accustomed to Jewish phrases about God's gift of life as his 'reign' or 'kingdom'.

It was true that people could not yet know and live *fully*. We are still confined, still waiting with longing for the final victory of life over death. But even so, we wait for it in hope because we already know it, experience it, even in our present unsatisfactory condition. Paul called this experience the 'first-fruits' of the life of the spirit, which is the *real* life. First-fruits are 'samples' of the harvest—they prove there *is* a harvest, but it isn't all gathered yet.

> For the creation waits with eager longing for the full revealing of God's sons [he means human beings, who share the life of God, just as sons are the same 'kind' of people as their father] for the creation was subjected to futility [i.e. was without apparent meaning or purpose] not of its own will but by the will of him who subjected it in *hope*, because creation itself will be set free from its slavery to decay and come to the glorious freedom of the children of God.

('Children of God' is the same sort of phrase as 'children of Israel'—it means people who are united by sharing in *one* life—in this case God's life, not simply a racial heritage.)

> We know that the whole creation has been groaning and labouring together until now—and not only the rest of creation but even ourselves, who have the 'first-fruits' of the Spirit, groan inwardly as we await the 'adoption' of sons, the redemption of our bodies.

Here is the distinctively Christian message. It is the *whole* human being, not just his 'soul' that achieves new life, and although we can't realize it fully yet we do really experience it, here and now.

There is one other thing about the Christian good news that made it (and makes it) entirely different from any other of the thousands of ways of salvation that men have sought and preached. Just as the apostles appealed to a real personal knowledge and experience in their hearers, they also appealed to a real, verifiable historical *event* as the proof and foundation of their message. They were not revealing a purely 'spiritual' (in the gnostic sense of 'unbodily') mystery. It was not a doctrine about a god-like hero or even a god in human form, whose death and resurrection was a symbol of the liberation his followers could attain. There were plenty of cults of this kind—of Osiris, Adonis, Mithras and many more. They all referred to a timeless and sometimes place-less event, a myth event, though obviously an important one.

The Christian proclamation was different. The story of Christ's death and resurrection certainly shows many points of similarity with these myths—naturally, for they are about the same thing, the longing of man for real life, and about how it is to be achieved. But the apostles did not explain it like that. They kept on pointing to an actual, dateable happening. 'Christ is risen,' they said 'and *we are witnesses* to it.' 'We saw it, we touched him,' they kept saying.

> That which was from the beginning, which we have heard, which we have seen with our eyes, which we have looked upon and touched with our hands, the Word of Life itself is what we are preaching. It was clearly shown, and we *saw* it, and we bear witness to it, and proclaim to you the eternal life which was

> with the Father and was made visible to us. What we are proclaiming to you is what we have *seen* and *heard* so that you may have fellowship with us; and our fellowship is with the Father and with his son, Jesus Christ. We are writing this to make our own joy complete.

This is from the Epistle of John, the writer of the fourth Gospel, and that Gospel is full of the same almost incredulous wonder. This is life *himself,* 'all things were made through him', he is the beginning and the end, Alpha and Omega—but also, he was *here*, we knew him, ate with him, chatted to him. We saw him die—and we saw him risen. 'We are witnesses of these things.' Paul, too, suddenly converted to the service of Christ from fierce and ardent Judaism, claimed to be a witness. It was this experience of encounter with Christ, risen and glorified, that converted him, and also made the substance and the power of his message ever after.

It is still the substance and power of the proclamation. Christianity stands or falls by this. 'If Christ has not been raised then our preaching is useless and your faith is useless,' wrote Paul to the Corinthians, who were wondering (as people have done ever since) what 'rising from the dead' could possibly mean, or whether it meant *anything.*

> We are even convicted of misrepresenting God, because we bore witness that God *did* raise Christ—whom he did not raise if it is true that the dead do

not rise. For if the dead cannot rise then Christ has not risen, your faith is futile and you are still in your sins. . . . But in fact Christ *has* been raised from the dead, the first-fruits of those who have 'fallen asleep'. For as death came by man, by a man also has come the resurrection of the dead. For as in Adam [he means the natural 'in the flesh' man] all die, so also in Christ shall all be made alive.

VIII

FROM DEATH TO LIFE

VIII

FROM DEATH TO LIFE

THE PROCLAMATION OF the risen Christ convinced thousands and later millions. They realized it as their way to life, accepted it, and lived by it. It was not a matter of reaching a reasoned conclusion about what was true, and deciding to live according to that truth. What was preached was true enough, but what happened to people who heard the message was not a change of opinion but a total personal revolution. It was conversion.

Conversion is a very odd sort of event. It isn't simply a huge emotional crisis, though such a crisis may be the way it happens. Conversion can be very quiet, and it can happen in stages, in lots of small 'conversions'. It doesn't mean just changing from one religion to another, or even from no religion to some religion, though such a change may be a conversion. For change of religion *can* be simply a change of opinion. Whatever form it takes it is obviously vital, if we are talking about finding life, since it means the breakthrough to a new experience of life.

In talking about this experience, which is crucial to the understanding of Christianity, it is easy to get so tangled up in metaphors—even obvious ones like using such words as 'freedom' and 'sacrifice'—that one loses touch with any kind of imaginable human happening. In the last chapter I tried to make clear by a sort of parable the kind of doctrine that the apostles preached, and why it was so effective. An explanation like that makes the idea easy to get hold of, intellectually, but doesn't produce conversion. It explains what is happening in the process we call by the short, hard words 'redemption' or 'salvation', but rather in the way that a map explains a country. It is an intelligible guide, but you know very well the real country doesn't look in the least like this. Nor, of course, can a map give any kind of experience of what it is like to *be* in that country.

I said earlier that the words and images that the apostles used in their preaching 'rang a bell' for their hearers. Unfortunately they seldom 'ring a bell' for us, unless we have learned to link them up with experiences of our own. The process is something like what happens when, for instance, someone mentions the name of a place you've been to, where you enjoyed yourself very much. The name is only the name of a house or a town —quite impersonal and 'neutral'. To anyone else who heard it it might be just a bit of geographical information—or not even that—a mere sound, a meaningless gabble. But to you it means memories, it means people you like, smells, sights, intimate jokes or shared discoveries, good food, the indescribable complex of experiences that make you realize 'I'm happy'. If you were happy there, and knew it, then every time you hear that word you feel that happiness again—perhaps rather sadly, because it is past and gone, or perhaps with excitement, because you hope to go back.

The words of the good news are words that work like this—that is why that rather terrifyingly compact statement of Paul's that I quoted on page 83 has the power to evoke, in people who have 'been there', the full experience of what they know. Yet to other people it seems meaningless or repulsive nonsense, or a formula to be accepted as holy, but too mysterious to be penetrated by the human mind.

Of course we can't fully penetrate it. It *is* mysterious, because it goes beyond the world of 'partly living' with its secure routines, its fully explainable behaviour, its safe and unchanging rules. But it is not mysterious in the sense that we know nothing about it at all, except what we are told by the tradition of the Church. In the third chapter I described the kind of experiences we think of as 'living' or 'real' and suggested why some of them were more 'really real' than others. These perfectly ordinary experiences are a clue to what is meant by 'salvation', the life to which conversion is the doorway.

There is an interesting sentence in another of Paul's

letters that ties up his teaching with what I said in the third chapter about human relationships as the most satisfying experience of 'liveness'. He uses his familiar terms; 'death' meaning the futile, sin-muddled, death-dominated existence we all know; 'life' meaning the freedom of the 'real self' (the spirit) which we know and experience incompletely, but know we 'possess' because this is experience of it. This is what he says: 'And so we have passed from death to life, *because we love the brethren.*'

It seems at first sight to contradict what he says so often, that the new life is discovered only by faith in Christ risen. Yet it isn't a contradiction, and it is by understanding *how* it isn't that we can get nearest to realizing how 'salvation' works, and how conversion happens.

In the Gospels Christ is often recorded as telling his hearers that only practical, active love shows that a man is right with God. It's no good saying 'Lord! Lord!', you have to *do* something, and the something is practical help to those who need it—this is love for him, Christ. 'I was hungry and you fed me, naked and you clothed me, sick and you visited me. . . .' In the parable, these blessed people ask, amazed, '*When* did we see you hungry and fed you, naked and clothed you?' And the answer is, 'Whatever you did for the least of my brethren, you did to me.' Love of the brethren *is* love of Christ. Paul himself says, 'If I have such faith that can move mountains, but lack charity, I am worth nothing.'

If service of others is truly love of Christ, what more can we want? Why the hammering away about faith, faith? 'Do you believe?' Christ asks people who come to him. 'Men of little faith!' he calls his disciples when they have let him down. 'Therefore we are justified [brought into right relationship with God] by *faith*, we have peace with God through our Lord Jesus Christ', writes Paul to the Romans.

What is this thing called faith? One minute Paul says it's essential, the next that it is no use without love. In the Gospels, Jesus calls men to faith in himself, but rejects those who do not show love for each other by practical service.

These two ideas have been argued over throughout the history of Christianity. They are the key ideas in the whole vision of life which we call Christian. How do they fit together?

The easiest way to think about this is to imagine a situation in ordinary life when the two things do work together. Doing this should make it possible to realize the meaning of a lot of the words that 'rang bells' for the first Christians, and often sound to us more like hitting plasticine.

Suppose that at school or college you were often with another person whom you didn't like much, a boy or a girl who was inclined to sulk, who seemed to resent remarks meant quite kindly, and who seldom said anything that wasn't sarcastic or offensive. Yet you had to work with this person, since you were expected to do quite a lot of things together—experiments in chemistry, for instance. And being the same age you were often together for meals and so on. What would you do? The normal reaction in a situation like this is to retreat into yourself. The other one seems locked in a kind of fortress of hostility, from which he only comes out in order to attack. In that case the obvious thing is to stay in a fortress of your own. You needn't be as disagreeable as the other is, of course. You can even make efforts to be considerate and polite, because you know that rows and bickering make life a misery for everyone. It takes some self-control not to answer back, but it can be done. If you manage to restrain your temper, you not unnaturally feel fairly pleased with yourself for not making a bad situation much worse. It would be much easier, after all, to let fly.

This imaginary but very common situation shows exactly what is meant by *sin* and *the Law*. People shut off, hostile, afraid of each other, resentful and suspicious—this is so common that we scarcely notice it. We notice it much less because most of the time the kind of behaviour that results from these feelings—rows, spitefulness or self-indulgence of various kinds as an escape from the dreariness of it all—these things are *controlled* by the Law. We learn, we are trained, to behave properly, to respect each other's property and persons, to be polite even when we don't feel like it. And it is because we learn 'this is wrong' and 'that is right' that we recognize which kinds of behaviour are 'anti-social'—contrary to the Law—and avoid them. Obviously this is necessary, the alternative would be such open bitterness and violence and self-indulgence that ordinary life would be impossible.

But in one way the sort of 'peaceful co-existence' that good behaviour 'according to the Law' makes possible is *worse* than open hostility. Although the Law is good and what it says is right *is* right (obviously, it *is* better to be kind than unkind), it can prevent any discovery of real relationship, real life between people. If you are very pleased with yourself for your self-control this will make it extremely hard for you to feel the least sympathy with your disagreeable neighbour. It may be better, in obvious ways, than retaliating, but it *shuts you in* just as much as resentment. Indeed, resentment is probably not far under the surface. If you are satisfied with yourself you don't see any point in trying to *change* the situation. You can live with it, and that's enough. But it is only 'partly living', what Paul calls 'death', and that is *all* that good behaviour—according to the Law—on its own can manage.

But suppose that you met someone, at a party perhaps, who knew your disagreeable companion, and knew his or her family background. This person might tell that the father was an alcoholic and constantly out of work, the mother worried and worn out and consequently always snapping at the children, so that home life was a nightmare. And your unbearable companion is the eldest, will probably have to support the others, and so will have to take any job going, missing the chance of further education and the career he or she really wanted. This throws an entirely different light on the affair. Anyone with a little imagination and not completely hard-boiled can realize that a family situation like this is enough to make anyone savage and cynical. Once you see this you are seeing a *person*. You are no longer looking at an object which is a nuisance to *you*, you see a human being struggling with an appalling problem and suffering very much. You *feel* this in yourself, and it hurts.

And what hurts even more is the sudden realization that your own behaviour, that seemed so courteous and civilized, was really completely callous, even brutal. Even a row might have relieved your companion's feeling of hopeless isolation. It would have been a *real* experience, a relationship of a kind—like the child who drives his mother to slap him rather than be ignored.

This new vision is horribly painful—it is as if a whole layer of yourself were being peeled off, and underneath you are raw and terribly sensitive. It is so unpleasant that you may want to cling to your old 'skin' of self-satisfaction, your protection of 'the flesh' strengthened and organized by 'the Law'. You say to yourself; 'I did at least try to behave decently, and after all, whatever the reasons, I did have a lot to put up with.' But if you are honest you know this is a sham. You may struggle against the new knowledge, but in the end you let it in. This is a decision, and it is a giving up of yourself, a leaving behind of the safe feeling you got from 'the Law'. You are taking a risk, you aren't—as far as you can see—going to get anything out of this but humiliation. But you do make the decision, you feel you *have* to, as if you were responding to an urgent invitation. This response is *faith*. Faith, then, lights up the whole situation. You see yourself for what you are, and this—though it is painful and shocking—sets you *free* from the old, tight 'skin' of self-control, into a new experience of life that you realize at once is real. This is what is meant by *repentance* and *conversion*—not just a decision to behave better, but the discovery of a new vision, a new *life*. And with it comes the awareness of what Paul called reconciliation. It isn't something that you can do or have, *after* you've repented. It is what real repentence *is*, when you really go through with it.

In the situation I have described it is quite possible that however much you wanted it, you wouldn't be able to bring about a reconciliation with the person you have wronged. He or she might feel too bitter about your former attitude to be able to believe that you had changed. But even so, there *is* reconciliation, in yourself. When you want to be reconciled with another person you are wanting to *share* something with them—be 'at one' with them *in* something, a sort of awareness of peace—or love or companionship or whatever you like to call it, that you already know, through faith, in yourself. It is because you know it yourself that you want to share it, for the fact that the other person doesn't seem to 'have' it or 'be in' it seems somehow all wrong. So the state of being reconciled or 'justified' isn't *just* the business of 'making up' a quarrel; rather, 'making up' becomes desirable because of the new awareness you have—an awareness of 'realness', of 'life'. The attitude to other people, the kind of approach to living that goes with this 'life' is what we call *love*. Because of what you discovered through the surrender of faith, because of your repentance and conversion and reconciliation, you love. Love is the *way of life* that shows the nature of the *life* you have discovered.

And you made this discovery because when you received the invitation to give up your 'old self' you said 'yes', even though it felt like giving up everything that made you feel safe, that gave you self-respect and a sense of right-doing. You were 'justified', in fact, by *faith*. But the new life you discovered in the self-giving of faith is a life of love and so you know at once that you must *do* something about what you now know, otherwise it will be a sham. The old way of being, the 'dead' way, has surrendered to life, and this came about because you realized someone else as a person to be loved, and it was this that presented you with the opportunity for the decision of faith, which lets love free to act—'and so we have passed from death to life, because we love the brethren'.

This example of salvation at work is a very small and ordinary one. It may seem far fetched to examine it in this elaborate way. But it really shows that salvation—the life with God that Christ offers—is going on all the time, it is *there*, under our hands, if only we will reach out and take it. This is what the first Christians realized, and rushed for. It is what Christians have been seeing ever since.

One more, rather difficult question arises. If this kind of thing is going on, even among people who have never heard of Christ, why do we need *him*? What is Christian about salvation?

There are two answers to this, and one could write several books about each, but a brief hint will give at least something to think about.

One is based on Christ's saying 'Whatever you did to the least of my brethren, you did to me.' *Any real* love is love of Christ, because he is the expression in human terms of what love is, which we 'touch' and 'live' by faith. To call him 'Son of God' is to try to express the fact that in him the principle of the universe, the creative 'thing' that shares, explodes, unites, transforms —in fact *God*—breaks through the surface of 'partly living' and becomes visible, touchable, *human*. And even when he is not seen he is *there*. So love, real self-giving, gives itself to him, *is* him. Anywhere, any time, in anyone.

The other answer is that the breakthrough of liveness that we call the incarnation shows us what is going on all around, though most of the time one isn't aware of it. It is the realization of love in Christ that makes people able to recognize love—Christ—and respond to it, wherever it occurs. Christ is not only the man who made the breakthrough in his own person, he is also—because of that—the sign and guarantee that *we* can do it. And because it is hard to do, and we'd much rather not, on the whole, we *need* this sign, this assurance of victory. The whole purpose of historical Christianity has been to display this sign to men, so they might pluck up courage and 'pass from death to life, because we love the brethren'.

IX

'THE TRADITION WHICH I RECEIVED—'

IX

'THE TRADITION WHICH I RECEIVED—'

AT THIS POINT, in thinking about Christianity as a revelation of life, we have to go back to the questions raised at the end of Chapter IV. They were questions about the *Church*, and its relation to the Christian message. Is Christianity the same as the Christian Church or Churches? Do we *need* a Church?

These questions are being asked more and more frequently and forcibly nowadays, and often the answer given to both is 'no'.

This is scarcely surprising. The impact of the Gospel message, described in the last chapters, was huge. It brought immediate recognition and response. It still does—because when people realize what the good news is about they recognize it as the answer to their deepest longings and half-felt hopes. It is clearly a message that can change people's lives entirely, and make them what Paul calls 'a new creation'. But granted all this—granted even that a real, constructive response to the message includes an understanding of the necessity of 'the Law' as background and framework of the new, free life—do we need a *Church*, an organized, compact group with clear-cut membership, officers, ceremonies, and so on?

Sometimes people who feel a Church is essential reply, 'but it's in the Bible—Christ founded a Church, and appointed the apostles to lead it. If Christ founded a Church that means Christianity *must* be a Church.' But it isn't so simple—there are certainly many texts in scripture that refer to the foundation of a Church, but when we go on to point to these as the justification of the Church *now* we are really assuming that the sort of thing we *now* call a Church is what was meant. We can see the Church as a historical fact, and we can see that it *did* grow from the apostles—but was the actual form it took really what Christ intended? Or did it happen to grow like that, for historical reasons, so that we now use 'hindsight' and *assume* this must have been what Christ intended?

And even supposing the kind of Church-structure that has come to us through the centuries *could* have been the kind of thing Christ intended, *has* it been? Considering the historical record of Christianity, isn't it time we recognized that however necessary a Church may have been in the past, it has so abused its origin that it has no longer any claim to respect? Was a Church ever a really *Christian* necessity, rather than a human political one? And if it has been, is it still?

If you have been brought up as a Christian and a

Church-member, these questions may seem rather shocking, perhaps ridiculous. But they are being asked, and asked by intelligent people, and above all by people of faith, who value the Christian message, and feel that the Church is an obstacle rather than a help to proclaiming it.

It is no use pretending that such people are merely ignorant, or lacking in trust in God, or asking too much of human nature. This is a serious challenge to the traditional idea of what Christianity is, indeed it is the most serious question that Christians are asking themselves in this generation. In the first chapter I said that in order to answer the question 'Why be a Christian?' one must be prepared to listen to doubts and look at facts honestly. So now, when the question is 'If I want to be a Christian need I belong to a *Church*?' I must be prepared to look as honestly as possible at the doubts and the facts. It isn't possible in a short book to give complete answers and arguments, or even all the facts. And in any case there *are* no final answers that can be given in a book. The decision must be reached in one's own private mind and heart, and the decision must be one about *love*. If what I have written in the last chapter means something, it means that Christianity is about the discovery and growth of real life, and that this life is a life of love. It is hard and painful, because selfishness feels safer, but it is an experience of liberation and joy on the other side of this pain. It is in relation to this realization of what Christ offers that we have to decide whether the message comes to us necessarily, or only accidentally, through a human organization, and *also* whether the carrying out of what Christian faith demands requires such an organization or not.

One thing needs to be clear, however. When we ask, Church or no Church? we are not asking whether the Church *in its present form* is the right tool for the proclamation of the good news. The Church—all the Churches—are changing and re-thinking themselves, some more, some less. So to look at a particular Church structure as it exists at present and say, Is *this* the best way to preach the Gospel? is really rather misleading. So the question divides itself into two—must there be a Church? And if the answer to this is 'yes' we must further ask 'Is the present organization of the Church adequate to the job, and if not *is it capable* of being so, or are its structures so stiff and antiquated that it can't be changed and should be scrapped?'

The simplest way to get a useful point of view on the whole question is to take a quick historical survey of Christianity, and see how the present situation arose.

I mentioned in chapter VI that the four Gospels were written because Christians no longer expected the end of all things any minute, and therefore felt the need of a more complete, leisurely account of what is sometimes called 'the Christ event'. They could study it and learn from it and grow in understanding through the years. This was one way of seeing that the message went on from the first generation to the next, and was not lost. This was also necessary because the apostles were getting older, some were already dead as martyrs, and the rest were always in danger of martyrdom. If the preaching of the Gospel was going to have to go on for a long time to come, then clearly it couldn't depend on the apostles. During their life-time, indeed right from the beginning, there had been leaders in each Christian community or 'Church', themselves usually appointed by the apostles. At first it was a flexible arrangement, the leader's main job being to 'preside', take the lead, when the community assembled to celebrate the Lord's Supper. This simple rite was the heart of the Christian communities, so the man who was 'president' at it obviously had a lot of influence. There were also 'elders'—respected and responsible men who made decisions, and settled quarrels, and so on. But as the original apostles died out and could no longer be consulted these leaders—*episkopoi*—naturally took over some of their work. They taught 'with authority', which means they demanded assent to what they taught because it came from the source, the *author* of the community, Christ, through the apostles. (If one thinks of authority as being a matter of 'referring to the author' it prevents a lot of misunderstanding. Authority is not the same as using power, though it may well *involve* the use of power.) What these *episkopoi* taught was 'the tradition we have received from the apostles', a phrase often used to settle arguments about what was, and was not, Christian truth. 'Tradition' means 'what is handed on'. The commission to preach the Gospel, first given to the apostles, was handed on (*traditus*) to their successors.

So, after this you get bishops, presiding over the eucharistic assembly in each community, and also *ruling* it, with the *authority* of the apostles, from Christ, the 'author'. For some time bishops were chosen or elected, which doesn't necessarily mean a ballot but public demand openly expressed in some way—sometimes by forcing the chosen man to accept consecration! But however they were appointed, they ruled and were the voice of the apostles.

Also, within a comparatively short time, the bishop of Rome was accepted as the leading bishop. Exactly how this primacy happened, and what it means, is in dispute, but the fact itself is undisputed.

From the very beginning there were disputes about what was the true teaching, and it so happens that the version supported by the Roman diocese always turned out in the end to be the one finally suported by the whole Church. But it is helpful to notice one fact when, nowadays, we think of the 'authority' (author-reference) of the Church as being a matter of pope and bishops, or at any rate clergy. The most important of all the early 'heresies' was the Arian one which split the Church for several centuries, led to wars, feuds and revolutions, and was supported by most of the Roman Emperors (who were Christians by then). During this time the vast majority of the bishops were Arians. Those who weren't were often exiled or in prison. What kept the 'tradition' alive? Who represented the authority of Christ? The answer is: the lay people, ordinary Christians.

The heart of the Church, geographically, was Rome, because that was the heart of the Empire. So when the emperors become Christian, the Empire became in a very nominal sense Christian—and the Church became a sort of Christian Roman Empire. It even adopted the court ceremonies of the Byzantine court (the emperors had moved to Byzantium) into its liturgy, and treated its bishops like Byzantine royalty. In the Catholic Church we still do, though this is changing. For the same reason, the priests and bishops of the Church were also servants of this Empire, in fact it was taken for granted that Christian meant *Roman*, for the civilized ideas on government, learning and so on that came from Rome were essential in order to create the political peace in which the Church could work. This was inevitable, but what happened was that the work of the Church as a political organism (which was necessary) came to seem the 'nature' of the Church.

At one stage the Eastern and Western parts of the Church developed a feud that was basically political. The two sides gave it a theological reason (though that could easily have been resolved) and the thing blew up into a major row that no diplomacy could heal. So the great schism happened in the ninth century, the first really big and lasting split in the Church.

The western or 'Roman' Church, under the pope, was supreme in Europe, and, nominally at least, everyone was Catholic. The Church provided all the learning there was, and secular government was supposed to be under the final authority of the pope. This did lead to peace and what is now called easy 'cultural exchange'. There was a huge intellectual ferment going on, but the Church as a political organism came more and more to be taken for granted, less and less likely to take a look at itself and 'seek first the kingdom of God'. Popes and bishops were too busy ruling, and patronizing the arts.

Since the official Church was to a great extent failing to preach the Gospel, people felt starved, and all through the middle ages there was a growing spiritual unrest that showed itself in things like the Crusades, in the popularity of the Franciscan friars vowed to poverty and simple proclamation of the Gospel, and the Dominicans, dedicated to truth and the Gospel, poor and single-minded.

There were also innumerable strange heretical sects, which were repressed with fierce brutality. The heresy-hunting and wars against heretics (in which the Catholic leaders made a lot of money) grew in horror and intensity as time went on. Attempts at reform there were, but the official Church was too rigid and too self-satisfied—and too rich—to allow really radical reform. So there came the Reformation.

This really was a theological split though there were strong political reasons for it also. The Reformers felt that the Roman Church had deprived Christians of the freedom of Christ. It was a Church of *Law*, in which rules were everything, behaviour the test of Christianity, ritual the way to ensure salvation. They felt it was a way of life from which the life had departed, it was all 'works' and no 'faith'. The Catholic Church, in return, emphasized the necessity of obedience and good works, the importance of *authority*, coming from the apostles and giving the bishops the right to teach with certainty. Tradition, the handing on of the message, came to mean that not only the message but *the method of handing it on* must be itself handed on, unaltered, from the past. And the past meant the medieval form —in its ritual, in its formulas of belief, in its official organization. And it set very hard indeed.

Meanwhile the Reformed Churches were more flexible, they could afford to experiment, to listen to the voice of inspiration which had been somewhat limited in the Church by political power. They realized that authority (reference to the author) was in the individual heart, as well as in the community's officers. Of course, in fact, both 'sides' recognized *two* kinds of authority— the voice of God in the tradition of the Church, proclaimed by her ministers, and the voice of God in the human heart. But each emphasized one only, to the point where the other was, in practice, unimportant and even suspect. So the Reformed tradition—it really *was* a tradition because any teaching has to be 'handed on' —was generally more spontaneous, gave more scope to ordinary people. But because of the weakness of the idea of authority through the organism it tended to split up. As time went on there were more and more Reformed Churches, sometimes almost as violently opposed to each other as to Catholicism. Anglicanism, in course of time, managed a rather successful compromise. It was traditional by its Englishness, mainly, while remaining theologically varied and even vague. It definitely had and has a tradition, and an official structure to teach it, but it has never grown as rigid as Catholicism.

Also there were religious wars, persecutions, tortures, heresy hunts, feuds, malice, gossip, bigotry, 'crusades', oppression, callous disregard for human happiness or even life. On both sides. All in the name of Christ. The long tale of Christian crimes, from the very beginning, has marked the existence of Christianity.

But then came the 'enlightenment', when men began to feel they'd had enough—if this was Christianity they could do without it. And then the advance of science seemed to make Christian teaching look like a lot of lies. The progressive, the forward-looking, felt that the Church (any Church) was a survival of the middle ages that must soon fade out as reason and science became able to provide an explanation of man and a hope for his future.

Under this massive challenge the Churches began to look at themselves and realize the sort of picture they presented. They began to be ashamed, but took some time to admit it. They saw themselves as traitors to Christ, because of their divisions, their smugness, their power-seeking, their indifference to suffering, their timid clinging to the old ways because the new ones threatened their possession of political influence. Little by little, reform began. Individuals, movements demanded change, demanded a new sense of mission, a response to the needs of people now.

First the Reformed Churches got together in the World Council of Churches, hoping and studying for re-union. They emphasized social responsibility, the Christian's mission of healing and peace. They questioned everything from vestments to the Trinity. Christianity began to look as if it might have something to say to the twentieth century.

Finally the most surprising thing of all: the bubbling of desire for renewal, the need to live and to love, finally broke through the centuries old surface of the Catholic Church. There was Pope John, there was the Council, the unchanging Church began to change.

The huge challenges that all the Churches are facing have thrown their whole way of life into confusion. Some people want to abandon the past and rush ahead, others want to cling to old forms that seem to provide security and clear values. There are disputes and despairs, experiments and exasperations, people leave the Church, rush into it, abuse it, embrace it, reject it, love it. This is where we are now. It's exciting, but worrying. This is the Church as we know it. These are the kind of effects which the Gospel message is having on people now, these are the ways in which people are reacting to the tradition—to that which has been handed on. It has come to us, handed on from one to another, through successive 'authorities'—bishops in the Catholic Church and in some other Churches—or clergy, ministers, elders of some kind. What is happening is because of the tradition, it stems from authority—the authority or 'authorship' of Christ.

X

CHRISTIANITY NOW: WHAT COMES NEXT?

X

CHRISTIANITY NOW: WHAT COMES NEXT?

THE SITUATION OF a Christian at this time is different from any previous one. In order to make sense of this one has to look back at the past situation.

In the past, as the last chapter showed, to be a Christian meant to belong to a Church of some kind—even if it called itself an assembly, a meeting, a fellowship, in order to avoid the 'authoritarian' overtones of the word 'Church'. Whatever it was called it was a body with a recognizable membership. And it had authority: that is it claimed to have Christ as its author. It also had tradition: that is it had received its teachings from somewhere, and was handing them on to the next generation of members. Many Christian bodies acknowledge the Bible alone as their authority, but in practice their understanding of it is conditioned by the kind of community they are, and who founded it. Their authority may come from scripture, in the sense that this is the revelation of Jesus Christ, their 'author' as Christians, but the way by which they 'refer back' to their author, as found in scripture, depends on the way they think of themselves as Christians. And that depends on the kind of organization they have, the way its teaching is done—by ministers, or by study in common, or from personal inspiration. For instance, a group that believes in personal inspiration as the source of authority will emphasize the bits about this in scripture and play down or ignore the bits about obedience and tradition. A group that has a strong central 'government' will explain away references to inspiration and 'gifts of the Spirit', and emphasize authority.

So even in groups that have no ministry at all there is authority, in the sense of a particular method of 'referring back' to their author. There is also tradition, because this 'method' is what makes the community what it is, and so is handed on down the years in order to keep it that way.

Authority and tradition, then, are the things that make *any* community a community at all. It has a *reason for being*, its authorship, whether it be a person, or a book or an ideal. This is its source, to which it refers back in order to keep its feeling of community, and to settle differences about what kind of community it is, and how it should behave.

You hear people say 'in *our* family we do this' or 'in *our* firm we don't do that'. And this really means that to behave some other way is to show you don't really belong, or don't want to. This is authority, and whoever has the right to do so may sometimes *enforce* the behaviour that shows you belong; or it may be discussed and decided on, or it may be so clearly sensible that anyone can see it's a good idea. *Or* it may be so stupid or inhuman that anyone can see you shouldn't do it—and in that case the community must either break up or reform. But, good or bad, vague or strict, it is authority, and the behaviour that shows it, that makes a community. And the same goes for tradition, which is simply the fact that the community *continues* to refer itself to its source.

But the *way* it refers back, the *method* by which authority works and tradition is made is not the same as the source, or the message. When we talk about 'traditional' customs or teaching we often mean both the message *and* the way it is explained and handed on. 'Traditionalists' are people who think we should continue to use the same methods to hand on the message. It is important to realize this, because, in fact, there is no dispute about the need to hand on the message—the only question is how.

And this is where we come up against the thing that makes our situation an entirely new one. For the first time in history it is possible to think of being a real Christian and not belonging to a Church. (There have been some in the past who said 'I'm as good a Christian as another, but I don't belong to any Church', but they usually meant that they reckoned they *behaved* as well as lots of Christians they knew, or knew of. Maybe they were right, but they weren't talking of being a Christian as the complete response to the Gospel message about faith and love.) It is possible now to think of groups of people meeting together unofficially, celebrating the Eucharist, doing their best to preach the Gospel and *live* it, in whatever work or place they happened to be. This is an idea that many find attractive. No authority to bully and restrict, no tradition to stifle initiative.

But the point is, as soon as you have a community dedicated to a single cause you have authority. And it gets its ideas from somewhere and hands them on. You have tradition. You have an assembly, a fellowship, you have a *Church*. But perhaps, even if it is a Church, in a sense, it is better to have this unofficial kind of Church, not owing allegiance to any particular tradition of Christian teaching?

To answer this we would have to discuss the idea of what the Church *is* in much more detail than there is room for here. But there are certain points that make it seem that it is not only possible but more *truthful* to take tradition as it comes, through the Church in the 'old' sense. For one thing any 'unofficial' Church gets its ideas from where all Christians do: 'the tradition entrusted to the apostles', in scripture and by word of mouth. And this has come to us through the Church of the past, corrupt and politically minded and brutal though it often was in its behaviour. To reject this history, because much of it is shameful, is like accepting an inheritance but refusing to acknowledge your heredity. Your family may be a poor lot, but they *are* your family. You may do better than they did, but in that case you are reforming your family. Even if you say they aren't yours. This is simply the fact—you can't *get rid of* your heredity, though you can disown it. The Church now—*any* Church now, however casual and unofficial—has grown straight out of the Church founded on the apostles. It may disown its heredity, it cannot avoid it.

But should we want to? Granted all the horrors, and the less exciting things like petty dishonesty and power-seeking, can we say that *all* the Church has done is to preserve a message for *us* to respond to? Have the centuries between contributed nothing?

Even to ask the question is to show that this is an unrealistic suggestion. There have been countless people who responded wholeheartedly to Christ—not only the heroism of the canonized saints lights up the Christian centuries, but the quiet goodness of thousands of unknown people who heard the message and lived it and brought it to others. One could say 'Yes, they heard the message and responded—this is nothing to do with the Church, except as a "messenger".' But it isn't *that* kind of message. It *can't* be passed on in words only. If these Christians who really lived their faith brought it to others they did so chiefly by *living* it. The Word of God is not just a spoken or written word, it is *lived* Word, a whole expression of what God is. *This* is the message, and nothing less.

In that case it is clear that the Church could not even have handed down the message unless it had been lived. Not just now and then, but all the time, down the centuries. Generation after generation 'heard' the Word, because they saw and felt and lived with it, as the apostles did with Christ. They saw it and heard it in people, in the way of life of Christianity, in its sacraments and services, and also in the everyday lives of Christians—in all this they saw Christ.

> . . . that which we have *heard*, which we have *seen* with our eyes, which we have looked upon and *touched* with our hands—the Word of life itself.

That was the message they heard, and they handed it on in the same way. They lived it. This, and not just 'teachings', is our tradition, our inheritance. It is a tradition of living, a new creation. It has never ceased, throughout all the distortions and sins, because life is stronger than death, love is stronger than fear, Christ is stronger than evil.

Paul of Tarsus was a strange, wild man, quick-tempered, intolerant, sometimes unjust, always domineering. There was plenty of evil in his own character and he knew it. There was plenty of evil in the Church, even then, and he knew it. But he also knew these things could not prevent the work of Christ, and sometimes when he thought of this it overcame him and his letters ceased to be explanations or instructions and became a sort of shout of exultation. There is one bit in his letter to the Roman Church which says a lot that is relevant for Christians now, when we are so conscious not only of enemies outside but of doubts inside and shame for the past and fears for the future. What *is* the Church coming to, we wonder. Is there a future for Christianity? We can't see ahead, all is uncertain and dark. We may have doubts about our own personal faith, and doubts about the future of Christianity. Yet, if the Gospel message is the message of life—does all this matter?

> 'If God is for us,' says Paul, 'what can it matter who is against us? It is God who makes us holy, so who can condemn us? Will Jesus Christ, he who died for us—yes, and was raised from the dead, he who is "at God's right hand" as our "representative"? In that case, what can possibly separate us from the love of Christ? Can disaster or sorrow, or persecution, or famine, or nakedness, or danger, or war? As it says in scripture—"for thy sake we are being killed every day—we are treated as sheep to be slaughtered." No—it is through things like this that we are able to triumph, by the power of him who loved us. For I am sure that neither death nor life, nor supernatural powers nor earthly powers, nor height nor depth, nor anything else in all creation will be able to separate us from the love of God which is shown to us in Christ Jesus our Lord.'

'Nor anything else in all creation—' which includes the human organization of the Church, if it happens to be feeble or worldly, or worse. Hate and sorrow and persecution and war have come through the sins of Christians, but they can't prevent the work of Christ. If *God* can forgive these things, through the love made visible and touchable in Christ, are we so arrogant that we can refuse forgiveness? If Christ does not condemn, can we? For Christ *is* encountered in the Church, otherwise there would be no message to hand on, he is present as he was in the manger and on the cross—and when he rose from the dead. The evidence of his presence is there, in the lives of those who have known his love and who live by it and live it. He does not condemn, but he said to the woman taken in adultery—'sin no more'. That is the message to us, who have inherited a very mixed tradition, a heritage of great glory and great shame. What the Church becomes, now, is up to us. We don't know what it will be like. We pray that it will be *one* Church, with old divisions forgotten. If all the various traditions of Christianity finally come together obviously the result will be something very different from any of the Churches we have at present. It isn't a question of compromise, it's a question of discovering the kind of 'way of life' that the tradition needs *now* in order to bring life to those who need it. What kind of community is the Church? What, from the past, is essential because it is part of what human communities just naturally are, and what was an adjustment to needs that have changed? These are the questions the Churches have to work out—not so as to feel cosier together, but because the Church has work to do, and disunity prevents it. We can't foresee all the answers, we can only work for them by following the truth and living the Gospel.

For the life of the Church is its message. Like Christ, the Church (whatever form it takes) is the Word of God for men. This Word, this message, is about life, it is the assurance that there is a meaning in human existence, and this meaning is love.

The Church means all the people who, by choice or accident, have come into the fellowship of those who are called to do Christ's work. And this work is to be a kind of prophet. A prophet is someone who is called to tell his own people who they are, and what is their destiny, when they have forgotten these things. As the prophets of Israel did this for their people, so the Church's work is to be a prophet for the whole human race. It has to remind people that human beings are holy, are able to live, not just exist, and that this life is eternal.

Eternal life doesn't mean 'life going on for ever' as if there were another huger kind of 'time' or even 'non-time' that we entered after death. It is of course impossible, really, to *think* about eternal life except in images, because our brains aren't eternal, and they are what we think with. But since we *do* think about it, whether we properly can or not, we use images, and an image that gives a better idea of what eternal life is about is that it is the 'inside' of the experience of liveness which we already know. If you can think of the most tremendous experience of liveness and realness you have ever known, and then think of getting *inside* that, so that you know it as your own 'country' and normal existence, that gives a hint of what eternal life means. Life to the nth, pure livingness. This is about as near as one can get with words, but some people seem able to get nearer to it than imagination can, as if in them the little 'cracks' in the skin of 'partly-living' were wider, or they learned to widen them, and know much more than most of us do of what it means. But they have never been able to tell other people what it is like. We still have to rely on a bit of imagination, and a lot of love.

For it is love, the real self-giving of faith, that makes people sure that human life *is* life. And the Church's work is to give people the courage to make that self-surrender into death, through which they come to life. And the way to do this is the way Christ did it—to love them, and by that love show them Christ's love, so that they can know him—see him, hear him, touch him, the Word of Life.

This is what Christians are called to do, now, and this is what you take on if you take on the Christian mission. In many ways it is harder now than it ever was. It is harder because most people don't believe, and never will. (It is partly the Christian sins and stupidities that have made Christian words meaningless to so many.) Yet these people who do not believe still need and crave life. They need Christ as much as ever. The Gospel must be preached to them, also—Christ told his Church to teach all nations—and most of the nations are not Christian, many not believers in God at all.

But the Gospel is a Word of love—not just a spoken or written word but a whole language of action. Words go with it—we must never stop proclaiming Christ in every way possible in words—but the crucial thing is action, for without this the words are empty. The prophet stands up before his people, who are so interested in their own cleverness and their own goodness that they can see nothing but what they have made, and says 'Behold your God'. He is here, in your experience of love and happiness, in your experience of grief and compassion, in your awareness of things, he is between the skin and the flesh, between the thought and the word. We must say it in a language people can understand, or what use is it? And for every age and every culture there is a new language. Yet it is not new, either. 'Feed the hungry, visit the sick, comfort the bereaved—' it is fairly familiar. It is the language of love.

Because of the way we use the word, 'love' sometimes begins to seem a mushy sort of thing, it can mean anything, and consequently nothing. This is why it is sometimes a dangerous word to use about the Christian life. It makes it sound sweet, patient, kind, and so on. A loving person can be all these things: must be, sometimes. But you have only to think of what people feel like when they are violently *in* love to realize that love is not a quiet thing. It isn't a kitten, it's a lion. Christian love, contrary to popular belief, is not less violent but more. You don't convert thousands, as Paul personally did, by being gentle and patient, yet he could be, if obliged to, if *that* was the way to get through to people and make them hear the message and live. Because love is about breaking down barriers, and that is hard and requires violence, though the violence may be directed at oneself. Crucifixion is a very violent affair.

A Christian is a person in love, a person dedicated to death, a person alive because of that. He is committed to breaking down barriers between people, and he does it 'out of' a community that knows that its life is shared, and from this sharedness (which is life in Christ) it draws its ideals and its signs and its power—its way of life that testifies to life. And when it doesn't testify the Christian is also pledged to do something about *that*.

Why be a Christian? Because by believing in all sincerity you come into a true relation with God, by saying and acting on your belief you find salvation. Then, scripture says:

> Those who believe in him will have no cause for shame, it makes no distinction between Jew and Greek—*all* men belong to the same Lord, who is rich enough, however many ask his help! For everyone who calls on the name of the Lord will be saved.
>
> But they will not ask for help unless they believe in him, and they will not believe in him unless they have heard of him, and how are they to hear without a preacher? And how can men preach unless they are sent? (As the scripture says, 'how beautiful are the feet of them that proclaim the good news!')
>
> So faith comes from what is heard, and what is heard is the proclamation of the word of Christ.

This is the reason for being a Christian: because God has called us to proclaim the good news of life, the word of Christ which is the Word of eternal life, that is proclaimed in truth, heard by faith, answered by love.